A Short History of Wales

A Short History of Wales

By

Owen Edwards

Enhanced Media
2016

A Short History of Wales by Owen Edwards. First published in 1906.

This edition published 2016 by Enhanced Media.

Enhanced Media Publishing
Los Angeles, CA.

First Printing: 2016.

ISBN-13: 978-1530734429

ISBN-10: 1530734428

Contents

CHAPTER I: WALES

Wales is a row of hills, rising between the Irish Sea on the west and the English plains on the east. If you come from the west along the sea, or if you cross the Severn or the Dee from the east, you will see that Wales is a country all by itself. It rises grandly and proudly. If you are a stranger, you will think of it as "Wales"—a strange country; if you are Welsh, you will think of it as "Cymru"—a land of brothers.

The geologist will tell you how Wales was made; the geographer will tell you what it is like now; the historian will tell you what its people have done and what they are. All three will tell you that it is a very interesting country.

The rocks of Wales are older and harder than the rocks of the plains; and as you travel from the south to the north, the older and harder they become. The highest mountains of Wales, and some of its hills, have crests of the very oldest and hardest rock—granite, porphyry, and basalt; and these rocks are given their form by fire. But the greater part of the country is made of rocks formed by water—still the oldest of their kind. In the north-west, centre, and west—about two-thirds of the whole country,—the rocks are chiefly slate and shale; in the south-east they are chiefly old red sandstone; in the north-east, but chiefly in the south, they are limestone and coal.

Its rocks give Wales its famous scenery—its rugged peaks, its romantic glens, its rushing rivers. They are also its chief wealth—granite, slate, limestone, coal; and lodes of still more precious metals—iron, lead, silver, and gold—run through them.

The highest mountain in Wales is Snowdon, which is 3,570 feet above the level of the sea. For every 300 feet we go up, the temperature becomes one degree cooler. At about 1,000 feet it becomes too cold for wheat; at about 1,500 it becomes too cold for corn; at about 2,000 it is too cold for cattle; mountain ponies graze still higher; the bleak upper slopes are left to the small and valuable Welsh sheep.

There are three belts of soil around the hills—arable, pasture, and sheep-run—one above the other. The arable land forms about a third of the country; it lies along the sea border, on the slopes above the Dee and the Severn, and in the deep valleys of the rivers which pierce far inland,—the Severn, Wye, Usk, Towy, Teivy, Dovey, Conway, and Clwyd. The pasture land, the land of small mountain farms, forms the middle third; it is a land of tiny valleys and small plains, ever fostered by the warm, moist west wind.

Above it, the remaining third is stormy sheep-run, wide green slopes and wild moors, steep glens and rocky heights.

From north-west to south-east the line of high hills runs. In the north-west corner, Snowdon towers among a number of heights over 3,000 feet. At its feet, to the north-west, the isle of Anglesey lies. The peninsula of Lleyn, with a central ridge of rock, and slopes of pasture lands, runs to the south-west. To the east, beyond the Conway, lie the Hiraethog mountains, with lower heights and wider reaches; further east again, over the Clwyd, are the still lower hills of Flint.

To the south, 30 miles as the crow flies, over the slate country, the Berwyns are seen clearly. From a peak among these—Cader Vronwen (2,573 feet), or the Aran (2,970 feet), or Cader Idris (2,929 feet)—we look east and south, over the hilly slopes of the upper Severn country.

Another 30 miles to the south rises green Plinlimmon (2,469 feet); from it we see the high moorlands of central Wales, sloping to Cardigan Bay on the west and to the valley of the Severn, now a lordly English river, on the east.

Forty miles south the Black Mountain (2,630 feet) rises beyond the Wye, and the Brecon Beacons (2,910 feet) beyond the Usk. West of these the hills fade away into the broad peninsula of Dyved. Southwards we look over hills of coal and iron to the pleasant sea-fringed plain of Gwent.

On the north and the west the sea is shallow; in some places it is under 10 fathoms for 10 miles from the shore, and under 20 fathoms for 20 miles. Tales of drowned lands are told—of the sands of Lavan, of the feast of drunken Seithenyn, and of the bells of Aberdovey. But the sea is a kind neighbour. Its soft, warm winds bathe the hills with life; and the great sweep of the big Atlantic waves into the river mouths help our commerce. Holy-head, Milford Haven, Swansea, Newport, Barry, and Cardiff—now one of the chief ports of the world—can welcome the largest vessels afloat. The herring is plentiful on the west coast, and trout and salmon in the rivers.

CHAPTER II: THE WANDERING NATIONS

By land and by sea, race after race has come to make the hills of Wales its home. One race would be short, with dark eyes and black hair; another would be tall, with blue eyes and fair hair. They came from different countries and along different paths, but each race brought some good with it. One brought skill in taming animals, until it had at last tamed even the pig and the bee; another brought iron tools to take the place of stone ones. Another brought the energy of the chase and war, and another a delight in sailing a ship or in building a fortress.

One thing they had in common—they wandered, and they wandered to the west. From the cold wastes and the dark forests of the north and east, they were ever pushing west to more sunny lands. As far back as we can see, the great migration of nations to the west was going on. The islands of Britain were the furthest point they could reach; for beyond it, at that time, no man had dared to sail into the unknown expanse of the ocean of the west. In the islands of Britain, the mountains of Wales were among the most difficult to win, and it was only the bravest and the hardiest that could make their home among them.

The first races that came were short and dark. They came in tribes. They had tribal marks, the picture of an animal as a rule; and they had a strange fancy that this animal was their ancestor. It may be that the local nicknames which are still remembered—such as "the pigs of Anglesey," "the dogs of Denbigh," "the cats of Ruthin," "the crows of Harlech," "the gadflies of Mawddwy"—were the proud tribe titles of these early people. Their weapons and tools were polished stone; their hammers and hatchets and adzes, their lance heads and their arrow tips, were of the hardest igneous rock—chipped and ground with patient labour.

The people who come first have the best chance of staying, if only they are willing to learn; hardy plants will soon take the place of tender plants if left alone. The short dark people are still the main part, not only of the Welsh, but of the British people. It is true that their language has disappeared, except a few place-names. But languages are far more fleeting than races. The loss of its language does not show that a race is dead; it only shows that it is very anxious to change and learn. Some languages easily give place to others, and we say that the people who speak these languages are good linguists, like Danes and Slavs. Other languages persist, those who speak them are unwilling to speak any new language, and this is the reason why Spanish and English are so widespread.

After the short dark race came a tall fair-haired people. They came in families as well as in tribes. They had iron weapons and tools, and the short dark people could not keep them at bay with their bone-tipped spears and flint-headed arrows. We know nothing about the struggle between them. But it may be that the fairy stories we were told when children come from those far-off times. If a fairy maiden came from lake or mound to live among men, she vanished at once if touched with iron. Is this, learned men have asked, a dim memory of the victory of iron over stone?

The name given to the short dark man is usually Iberian; the name given to the tall fair man who followed him is Celt. The two learnt to live together in the same country. The conqueror probably looked upon himself at first as the master of the conquered, then as simply belonging to a superior race, but gradually the distinction vanished. The language remained the language of the Celt; it is called an Aryan language, a language as noble among languages as the Aran is among its hills. It is still spoken in Wales, in Brittany, in Ireland, in the Highlands of Scotland, and in the Isle of Man. It was also spoken in Cornwall till the eighteenth century; and Yorkshire dalesmen still count their sheep in Welsh. English is another Aryan tongue.

The more mixed a nation is, the more rich its life and the greater its future. Purity of blood is not a thing to boast of, and no great and progressive nation comes from one breed of men. Some races have more imagination than others, or a finer feeling for beauty; others have more energy and practical wisdom. The best nations have both; and they have both, probably, because many races have been blended in their making. There is hardly a parish in Wales in which there are not different types of faces and different kinds of character.

The migration is still going on. Trace the history of an upland Welsh parish, and you will find that, in a surprisingly short time, the old families, high and low, have given place to newcomers. Look into the trains which carry emigrants from Hull or London to Liverpool on their way west—they have the blue eyes and yellow hair of those who came two thousand years ago. But this country is no longer their goal, the great continent of America has been discovered beyond. Fits of longing for wandering come over the Welsh periodically, as they came over the Danes—caused by scarcity of food and density of population, or by a sense of oppression and a yearning for freedom. An empty stomach sometimes, and sometimes a fiery imagination, sent a crowd of adventurers to new lands. And it is thus that every living nation is ever renewing its youth.

CHAPTER III: ROME

It is not a spirit of adventure and daring alone that makes a nation. Rome rose to say that it must have the spirit of order and law too. It rose in the path of the nations; it built the walls of its empire, guarded by the camps of its legions, right across it. For four hundred years the wandering of nations ceased; the nations stopped—and they began to till the ground, to live in cities, to form states. The hush of this peace did not last, but the memory of it remained in the life of every nation that felt it. Unity and law tempered freedom and change.

The name of Rome was made known, and made terrible, through Wales by a great battle fought on the eastern slopes of the Berwyn. The Romans had conquered the lands beyond the Severn, and had placed themselves firmly near the banks of that river at Glevum and Uriconium. Glevum is our Gloucester, and its streets are still as the Roman architect planned them. Uriconium is the burnt and buried city beyond Shrewsbury; the skulls found in it, and its implements of industry, and the toys of its children, you can see in the Shrewsbury Museum.

The British leader in the great battle was Caratacus, the general who had fought the Romans step by step until he had come to the borders of Wales, to summon the warlike Silures to save their country. We do not know the site of the great battle, though the Roman historian Tacitus gives a graphic description of it. The Britons were on a hill side sloping down to a river, and the Romans could only attack them in front. The enemy waded the river, however, and scaled the wall on its further bank; and in the fierce lance and sword fight the host of Caratacus lost the day. He fled, but was afterwards handed over to the Romans, and taken to Rome, to grace the triumphal procession of the victors.

The battle only roused the Silures to a more fierce resistance, and it cost the Romans many lives, and it took them many years, to break their power. The strangest sight that met the invaders was in Anglesey, after they had crossed the Menai on horses or on rafts. The druids tried to terrify them by the rites of their religion. The dark groves, the women dressed in black and carrying flaming torches, the aged priests—the sight paralysed the Roman soldiers, but only for a moment.

Vespasian—it was he who sent his son Titus to besiege Jerusalem—became emperor in 69. The war was carried on with great energy, and by 78 Wales was entirely conquered.

Then Agricola, a wise ruler, came. The peace of Rome was left in the land; and the Welshman took the Roman, not willingly at first, as his teacher and ruler instead of as his enemy. Towns were built; the two Chesters or Caerlleons (Castra Legionum), on the Dee and the Usk, being the most important from a military point of view. Roads were made; two along the north and south coasts, to Carmarthen and Carnarvon; two others ran parallel along the length of Wales, to connect their ends. On these roads towns rose; and some, like Caerwent, were self-governing communities of prosperous people. Agriculture flourished; the Welsh words for "plough" and "cheese" are "aradr" and "caws"—the Latin aratrum and caseus. The mineral wealth of the country was discovered; and copper mines and lead mines, silver mines and gold mines, were worked. The "aur" (gold) and "arian" (silver) and "plwm" (lead) of the Welshman are the Latin aurum, argentum, and plumbum.

The Romans allowed the Welsh families and tribes to remain as before, and to be ruled by their own kings and chiefs. But they kept the defence of the country—the manning of the great wall in the north of Roman Britain, the garrisoning of the legion towns, and the holding of the western sea—in their own hand.

Gradually the power of Rome began to wane, and its hold on distant countries like Britain began to relax. The wandering nations were gathering on its eastern and northern borders, and its walls and legions at last gave way. It had not been a kind mother to the nations it had conquered—in war it had been cruel, and in peace it had been selfish and stern. The lust of rule became stronger as its arm became weaker. The degradation of slavery and the heavy hand of the tax-gatherer were extending even to Wales. The barbarian invader found the effeminate, luxurious empire an easy prey. In 410 Alaric and his host of Goths appeared before the city of Rome itself; and a horde of barbarians, thirsting for blood and spoil, surged into it. The fall of the great city was a shock to the whole world; the end of the world must be near, for how could it stand without Rome? Jerome could hardly sob the strange news: "Rome, which enslaved the whole world, has itself been taken."

Rome had taken the yoke of Christ; and many said that it fell because it had spurned the gods that had given it victory. Three years after Alaric had sacked it, Augustine wrote a book to prove that it was not the city of God that had fallen; and that the heathen gods could neither have built Rome in their love nor destroyed it in their anger. He then describes the rise of the real "City of God," in the midst of which is the God of justice and mercy, and "she shall not be moved."

CHAPTER IV: THE NAME OF CHRIST

The name of Christ had been heard in Britain during the period of Roman rule, but we do not know who first sounded it. There are many beautiful legends—that the great apostle of the Gentiles himself came to Britain; that Joseph of Arimathea, having been placed by the Jews in an open boat, at the mercy of wind and wave, landed in Britain; that some of the captives taken to Rome with Caratacus brought back the tidings of great joy.

We know that the name of Christ, between 200 and 300 years after His death, was well known in Britain, and that churches had been built for His worship. Between 300 and 400 we have an organised church and a settled creed. Between 400 and 500 there was searching of heart and creed, and heresies—a sure sign that the people were alive to religion. Between 500 and 600 there was a translation of the Bible from Hebrew and Greek into the better-known Latin. The whole of Wales becomes Christian; and probably St David converted the last pagans, and built his church among them.

Between 450 and 500 a stream of pagan Teutons flowed over the east of Britain, and the British Church was separated from the Roman Church. By 664 British and Roman missionaries had converted the English; and the two Churches of Rome and Britain, once united, were face to face again. But they had grown in different ways, and refused to know each other. Their Easter came on different days; they did not baptize in the same way; the tonsure was different—a crescent on the forehead of the British monk, and a crown on the pate of the Roman monk. In the Roman Church there was rigid unity and system; in the British Church there was much room for self-government. The newly converted English chose the Roman way, because they were told that St Peter, whose see Rome was, held the keys of heaven. Between 700 and 800 the Welsh gradually gave up their religious independence, and joined the Roman Church.

But there was another dispute. Were the four old Welsh bishoprics—Bangor, St Asaph, St David's, Llandaff—to be subject to the English archbishop of Canterbury, or to have an archbishopric of their own at St David's? By 1200 the Welsh bishoprics were subject to the English archbishop, and Giraldus Cambrensis came too late to save them.

But through all these disputes the Church was gaining strength. Churches were being built everywhere. Up to 700 they were called after the name of their founder; between 700 and 1000 they were generally dedicated to the archangel Michael—there are several Llanvihangels [1] in Wales; after 1000 new churches were dedicated to Mary, the Mother of Christ—we have many Llanvairs. [2]

Times of civil strife, or of popular indifference, came over and over again; and the old paganism tried to reassert itself. And time after time the name of Christ was sounded again by men who thought they had seen Him. In the twelfth century the Cistercian monk came to say that the world was bad, that prayer saved the soul, and that labour was noble. [3] He was followed by the Franciscan friar, who said that deeds of mercy and love should be added to prayer, that Christ had been a poor man, and that men should help each other, not only in saving souls, but in healing sickness and relieving pain. In the fifteenth century the Lollard came to say that the Church was too rich, and that it had become blind to the truth, and Walter Brute said that men were to be justified by faith in Christ, not by the worship of images or by the merit of saints. In the sixteenth century came the Protestant, and the sway of Rome over Wales came to an end; Bishop Morgan translated the Bible into Welsh, and John Penry yearned for the preaching of the Gospel in Wales. The Jesuit followed, calling himself by the name of Jesus, to try to win the country back again to Rome. Robert Jones toiled and schemed, and some laid down their lives. The Puritan came in the seventeenth century to demand simple worship, and Morgan Lloyd thought that the second advent of Christ was at hand. The Revivalist came in the eighteenth century, and, in the name of Christ, aroused the people of Wales to a new life of thought.

After all this, you will be surprised to learn that many of the old gods still remain in Wales, and much of the old pagan worship. Who drops a pin into a sacred well, or leaves a tiny rag on a bush close by, and then wishes for something? A young maiden in the twentieth century, who sacrifices to a well heathen god. Until quite recently men thought that Ffynnon Gybi, and Ffynnon Elian, and Ffynnon Ddwynwen, had in them a power which could curse and bless, ruin and save.

Lud of the Silver Hand was the god of flocks and ships. His caves are in Dyved still, and his was the temple on Ludgate Hill in London. Merlin was a god of knowledge; he could foretell events. Ceridwen was the goddess of wisdom; she distilled wisdom-giving drops in a cauldron. Gwydion created a beautiful girl from flowers, "from red rose, and yellow broom, and white anemony." I am not quite sure what Coil did, but I have heard children singing the history of "old King Cole." Olwen also walked through Wales in heathen times, and it is said that three white flowers rose behind her wherever she had put her foot.

CHAPTER V: THE WELSH KINGS

The spirit of Rome remained, though Rome itself had fallen. And Welsh kings rose to take the place of the Roman ruler, trying to force the tribes of Wales—of different races and tongues—to become one people.

The chief Roman ruler, at any rate during the later wars against the invaders, was called Dux Britanniae, "the ruler of Britain." It became the aim of the ablest kings to restore the power of this officer, and to carry on his work, to rule and defend a united country. And I will tell you briefly how the kings ruled and defended Wales for more than five hundred years—how Maelgwn tried to unite it, how Rhodri tried to prevent the attacks of Saxon and Dane, how Howel gave it laws, and how Griffith tried to defend it against England.

Between 400 and 450 Rome left Wales to look after itself. An able family, called the House of Cunedda, took the power of the Dux Britanniae, and they translated the title into Gwledig—"the ruler of a gwlad (country)." Of this family Maelgwn Gwynedd is the most famous. It was his work to try to unite all the smaller kings or chiefs of Wales under his own power as "the island dragon." It was a difficult thing to persuade them; they all wanted to be independent. A legend shows that Maelgwn tried guile as well as force. The kings met him at Aberdovey, and they all sat in their royal chairs on the sands. And Maelgwn said: "Let him be king over all who can sit longest on his chair as the tide comes in." But he had made his own chair of birds' wings, and it floated erect when all the other chairs had been thrown down. Before Maelgwn died of the yellow plague in 547, his strong arm had made Wales one united country, and had made every corner of it Christian.

The new wave of nations, coming on as surely as the tide, began to beat against Wales. The Picts came from the northern parts of Britain, and Teutonic tribes swarmed across the eastern sea. The Angles came to the Humber, and spread over the plains of the north and the midlands of Roman Britain; the Saxons came to the Thames, and won the plains and the downs of the south-east. In 577 the Saxons, after the battle of Deorham, pierced to the western sea at the mouth of the Severn; they crept up along the valley of the Severn, burning the great Roman towns. Before they reached Chester and the Dee, however, they were defeated at the battle of Fethanlea in 584. But the Angles soon appeared, from the north; and after their victory at Chester in 613, they won the plains right to the Irish Sea.

Wales was now surrounded on the land side by a people who spoke strange languages, and who worshipped different gods, for the Angles and the Saxons were heathens. From the sea also it was open to attack. Sometimes the Irish came. But the most feared of all were the Danes, whose sud-sudden appearance and quick movements and desperate onslaughts were the terror of the age. The "black Danes" came from the fords of Norway, the "white Danes" from the plains of Sweden and Denmark. The Danes settled on the south coast: Tenby is a Danish name. Offa, the king of the Mercian Angles, took the rich lands between the Severn and the Wye; but Offa's Dyke (Clawdd Offa) is probably the work of some earlier people whose history has been lost. It was only by incessant fighting that the enemy could be kept at bay.

Of all the kings who tried to defend his country against the enemies which now stood round it, the greatest is Rhodri, called Rhodri Mawr—"the Great." From 844 to 877, by battles on sea and land, he broke the spell of Danish and Saxon victories; and his might and wisdom enabled him to lead his country in those dark days. Like Alfred of Wessex, who lived at the same time and faced the same task, he stemmed the torrent of Danish invasion and beat the sea-rovers on their own element. Like Alfred, he left warlike children and grandchildren. One of the grandsons was Howel the Good, who put the laws of Wales down in a book.

Wales and England were now, both of them in their own way, trying to become one country. It was seen by many that strength and peace were better than division and war. In England, the Earls of Mercia and Wessex tried to rise into supreme power. In Wales Llywelyn ab Seisyll, victorious in many battles and wishing for peace, made the country rich and happy. Still, when he died in 1022, the princes said they would not obey another over-king.

But the long ships full of Danes came again; the Angles crossed the Severn: war and misery took the place of peace and plenty. Griffith, the son of Llywelyn, came to renew his father's work. In the battle of Rhyd y Groes on the Severn, in 1039, he drove the Mercians back; in the battle of Pencader, in 1041, he crushed the opponents of Welsh unity; in 1044 he defeated the sea-rovers at Aber Towy. At the same time Harold, Earl of Wessex, was making himself king of England. A war broke out between Griffith and Harold; and, during it, in 1063, the great Welsh king—"the head and the shield of the Britons"—was slain by traitors.

CHAPTER VI: THE LAWS OF HOWEL

The two ideas which ruled Wales were—the love of order and the love of independence. The danger of the first is oppression; the dangers of the other are anarchy and weakness. Wales was sometimes united, under a Maelgwn or a Rhodri, and the princes obeyed them; oftener, perhaps, the princes of the various parts ruled in their own way.

The internal life of Wales is best seen in the laws of Howel the Good. Howel was the grandson of Rhodri; and, about 950, he called four men from each district to Hendy Gwyn (Whitland) to state the laws of the country. Twelve of the wisest put the law together; and the most learned scribe in Wales wrote it.

It was thought that there should be one king over the whole people, but it was very rarely that every part of Wales obeyed one king. The country was divided into smaller kingdoms. In many ways Gwynedd was the most powerful. It was very easy to defend; for it was made up of the island of Môn (Anglesey), the promontory of Lleyn, and the mountain mass of Snowdon. Its steep side was thus towards England, and its cornlands and pastures on the further side. It was also the home of the family of Cunedda, from Maelgwn to the last Llewelyn.

Powys was the Berwyn country. Ceredigion was the western slope of the Plinlimmon range; the eastern slopes had many smaller, but very war-like, districts. Deheubarth contained the pleasant glades and great forests of the Towy country. Dyved was the peninsula to the west; the southern slopes of the Beacons were Morgannwg and Gwent.

Howel the Good found that the laws of the various parts differed in details, and he gave different versions to the north, the south-west, and the south-east. But the law and life of the whole people, if we only look at important features, are one. Several commotes made a cantrev, many cantrevs made a kingdom, many kingdoms made Wales.

In each commote there were two kinds of people—the free or high-born, and the low-born or serfs. These may have been the conquering Celt and the conquered Iberian. It was very difficult for those in the lower class to rise to the higher; but, after passing through the storms of a thousand years, the old dark line of separation was quite lost sight of.

The free family lived in a great house—in the hendre ("old homestead") in winter, and in the mountain havoty ("summer house") in summer.

The sides of the house were made of giant forest trees, their boughs meeting at the top and supporting the roof tree. The fire burnt in the middle of the hall. Round the walls the family beds were arranged. The family was governed by the head of the household (penteulu), whose word was law.

The highest family in the land was that of the king. In his hall all took their own places, his chief of the household, his priest, his steward, his falconer, his judge, his bard, his chief huntsman, his mediciner, and others. The chief royal residences were Aberffraw in Môn, Mathraval in Powys, and Dynevor in Deheubarth.

Old Welsh law was very unlike the law we obey now.

The king was to be honoured. According to the laws of Gwynedd, if any one did violence in his presence he had to pay a great fine—a hundred cows, and a white bull with red ears, for every cantrev the king ruled; a rod of gold as long as the king himself, and as thick as his little finger; and a plate of gold, as broad as the king's face, and as thick as a ploughman's nail.

The judge, whether of the king's court or of the courts of his subjects, was to be learned, just, and wise. Thus, according to the laws of Dyved, was an inexperienced judge to be prepared for his great office; he was to remain in the court in the king's company, to listen to the pleas of judges who came from the country, to learn the laws and customs that were in force, especially the three main divisions of law, and the value of all tame animals, and of all wild beasts and birds that were of use to men. He was to listen especially to the difficult cases that were brought to the court, to be solved by the wisdom of the king. When he had lived thus for a year, he was to be brought to the church by the chaplain; and there, over the relics and before the altar, he swore, in the presence of the great officers of the king's court, that he would never knowingly do injustice, for money or love or hate. He is then brought to the king, and the officers tell the king that he has taken the solemn oath. Then the king accepts him as a judge, and gives him his place. When he leaves, the king gives him a golden chessboard, and the queen gold rings, and these he is never to part with.

Falconry was the favourite pastime of the kings and nobles of the time; indeed, everybody found it very exciting to watch the long struggle in the air between the trained falcon and its prey, as each bird tried every skill of wing and talon that it knew. The falconer was to drink very sparingly in the king's hall, for fear the falcons might suffer; and his lodging was to be in the king's barn, not in the king's hall, lest the smoke from the great fire-place should dim the falcon's sight.

CHAPTER VII: THE NORMANS

On the death of Griffith ap Llywelyn, many princes tried to become supreme. Bleddyn of Powys, a good and merciful prince, became the most important.

In January 1070, when the snow lay thick on the mountains, William, the Norman Conqueror, appeared at Chester with an army. He had defeated and killed Harold, the conqueror of Griffith ap Llywelyn, in 1066; he had crushed the power of the Mercian allies of Bleddyn; he had struck terror into the wild north, and England lay at his feet.

He turned back from Chester, but he placed on the borders a number of barons who were to conquer Wales, as he had conquered England. They had a measure of his ability, of his energy, and of his ambition.

The two great Norman traits were wisdom and courage; but the one was often mere cunning, and the other brutal ferocity. But no one like the Norman had yet appeared in Wales—no one with a vision so clear, or with so hard a grip. A hard, worldly, tenacious, calculating race they were; and they turned their faces resolutely towards Wales.

From England, Wales can be entered and attacked along three valleys—along the Dee, the Severn, and the Wye. At Chester, Hugh of Avranches, called "The Wolf," placed himself. From its walls he could look over and covet the Welsh hills, as he could have looked over the Breton hills from Avranches. He loved war and the chase: he despised industry, he cared not for religion; he was a man of strong passions, but he was generous, and he respected worth of character. One of his followers, Robert, had all his vices and few of his virtues. It was he who extended the dominions of the Earl of Chester along the north coast to the Clwyd, where he built a castle at Rhuddlan; and thence on to the valley of the Conway, where he built a castle at Deganwy. The cruelty of Robert shocked even the Normans of his time. He even set foot in Anglesey, which looked temptingly near from Deganwy, and built a castle at Aberlleiniog.

At Shrewsbury, where the Severn, after leaving the mountains of Wales, turns to the south, Roger of Montgomery was placed, with his wife Mabel, an energetic little woman, hated and feared by all. Roger himself, while ever ready to fight, preferred to get what he wanted by persuasion; he was not less cruel than Hugh of Chester, but he was less fond of war. He and his sons pushed their way up the Severn, and built a castle at Montgomery.

To Hereford, on the Wye, William Fitz-Osbern came. He was the ablest, perhaps, of all the followers of the Conqueror. He entered Wales; he saw it from the Wye to the sea, and he thought it was not large enough, and that it was too far from the political life of the time. So he went back to Normandy, but he left his sons William and Roger behind him. William had his father's wisdom. Roger had his father's recklessness in action; he rebelled against his own king, and found himself in prison. The king sent him, on the day of Christ's Passion, a robe of silk and rarest ermine. The caged baron made a roaring fire, and cast the robe into it. "By the light of God," said William the Conqueror, for that was his wicked oath, "he shall never leave his prison."

But another Norman, Bernard of Neufmarché, came to take his place. He built his castle at Brecon, and defeated and killed Rees, the King of Deheubarth; and, with great energy, he took possession of the upper valleys of the Wye and the Usk.

Further south William the Conqueror himself came to Cardiff, and possibly built a castle. The Norman conquest of the south coast of Wales was exceedingly rapid, and castle after castle rose to mark the new victorious advances—Coety, Cenfig, Neath, Kidwelly, Pembroke, Newport, Cilgeran.

So far, the Norman advance has been a most quick one. In less than twenty-five years from the appearance of the Conqueror at Chester, the whole country had been overrun except the mountains of Gwynedd and the forests of the Deheubarth. This success is easily explained.

For one thing, the Normans had trained, professional soldiers, who were well horsed and well armed. In a pitched battle the hastily collected Welsh levies, unused to regular battle and very lightly armed, had no chance.

Again, the Welsh opposition was not only not organised, but weakened by internal strife. While the Norman was winning valley after valley, the Welsh princes were trying to decide by the issue of battle who was to be chief. Bleddyn was slain in 1075; and his nephews and cousins tried to rule the country. Among these, Trahaiarn was a soldier of ability and energy, and a ruler of real genius. But he was the rival of the exiled princes of the House of Cunedda, and he found it difficult to bend Snowdon and the Vale of Towy to his will. Two of the exiles met him, probably near some of the cairns in the valley of the Teivy; and there, in the battle of Mynydd Carn, fiercely fought through the dusk into a moonlight night in 1079, Trahaiarn fell. It looked as if no leader could rise in Wales to fight a Norman army or to take a Norman castle.

CHAPTER VIII: GRIFFITH AP CONAN AND GRIFFITH AP REES

In the battle of Mynydd Carn, a young chief led the shining shields of the men of Gwynedd. He was Griffith, the son of a prince of the line of Cunedda and of a sea-rover's daughter. He was mighty of limb, fair and straight to see, with the blue eyes and flaxen hair of the ruling Celt. In battle, he was full of fury and passion; in peace, he was just and wise. His people saw at first that he could fight a battle; then they found he could rule a country. And it was he that was to say to the Norman: "Thus far shalt thou come, and no further."

When Bleddyn died in 1075, Griffith came to Gwynedd, and found that his father's lands were under new rulers. Robert of Rhuddlan and Trahaiarn of Arwystli were mighty foes; but Griffith drove both of them back; and, by his prowess and success in battle, broke the spell of conquest which kept Gwynedd in bonds. But his enemies attacked him again from all sides; and, while Hugh the Wolf and Robert of Rhuddlan were laying Gwynedd waste, Trahaiarn and Griffith met at the hard-fought battle of Bron yr Erw. Griffith lost the day, and again became a sea-rover. He sailed to Dyved, and there he met Rees, the King of Deheubarth, who also was of the line of Cunedda, and had been driven from his land by the Normans. The two chiefs joined, and they crushed Trahaiarn at Mynydd Carn. Then they turned against the Normans.

Rees soon fell in battle, and left two children, Nest and Griffith. The beauty of Nest and the genius of Rees ap Griffith fill an important page in the history of their country. Nest became the mother of the conquerors of Ireland; Rees became the greatest of all the kings of South Wales.

The Normans found that the Welsh had taken heart. Of their opponents, they feared three: Griffith ap Conan, Owen of Powys, and Griffith ap Rees. The kings of England, the two sons of the Conqueror—red, brutal William and cool, treacherous Henry—had to come to help their barons.

Griffith ap Conan had a long life of strife and success. In his struggle with Hugh the Wolf, he was once in The Wolf's prison, and more than once he had to flee to the sea. But, backed up by the liberty-loving sons of Snowdon and by his sea-roving kinsmen, he made Gwynedd strong and prosperous. He drove the Normans from Anglesey; he attacked and killed Robert of Rhuddlan; he saw the red King of England himself forced by storm and rain to beat a retreat from Snowdon. He was loved by his people during his youth of adventure and battle, and during his old age of safe counsel and love of peace. His wife Angharad and his son Owen live with him in the memory of his country. When he died, in 1137, it was said that he had saved his people, had ruled them justly, and had given them peace.

In the Severn country the princes of Powys were fighting against the Normans also, especially against the family of Montgomery. The sons of Bleddyn—Cadogan, Iorwerth, and Meredith—were driving the invaders from the valley of the Severn, and from Dyved, defeating their armies in battle, and storming their castles. Sometimes they would make alliances with them, and defy the King of England. But it is difficult to follow each of them. The history of one of them, Owen ap Cadogan, is like a romance. He was brave and handsome, in love with Nest, and a very firebrand in politics. The army of Henry I. was too strong for him, and he had to submit. He then became the friend of the King of England. It was the aim of the princes of Powys to be free, not only from the Norman, but also from Griffith of Gwynedd and Griffith of Deheubarth. They were an able and versatile family; noble and base deeds, revolting crimes and sweet poems, come in the stirring story of their lives.

What Griffith did in the north, and the sons of Bleddyn in the east, Griffith ap Rees did in the south; he showed that the Norman army could be beaten in battle, and that a Norman castle could be taken by assault. After his father's death he spent much of his youth in exile or in hiding: sometimes we find him in Ireland, sometimes in the court of Griffith ap Conan, sometimes with his sister Nest—now the wife of Gerald, the custodian of Pembroke Castle. But he had one aim ever before him—to recover his father's kingdom and to make his people free. Castle after castle rose—at Swansea, Carmarthen, Llandovery, Cenarth, Aberystwyth—to warn him that the hold of the Norman on the land was tightening. He came to the forests of the Towy; his people rallied round him, and his power extended from the Towy to the Teivy, and from the Teivy to the Dovey. His wife, the heroic Gwenllian—who died leading her husband's army against the Normans—was Griffith ap Conan's daughter. The great final battle between Griffith and the Normans was fought at Cardigan in 1136, in which the great prince won a memorable victory over the strongest army the Normans could put in the field. In 1137 he died, and they said of him that he had shown his people what they ought to do, and that he had given them strength to do it.

But, though the Norman was not allowed to bring his stone castle and cruel law, what good he brought with him was welcomed. The piety of the Norman, his intellectual curiosity, and his spirit of adventure, conquered in Welsh districts where his coat of mail and his castle were not seen.

CHAPTER IX: OWEN GWYNEDD AND THE LORD REES

The men who opposed the Normans left able successors—Owen Gwynedd followed his father, Griffith ap Conan; the Lord Rees followed his father Griffith ap Rees; and in Powys the sons of Bleddyn were followed by the castle builder Howel, and by the poet Owen Cyveiliog.

Owen Gwynedd ruled from 1137 to 1169; the Lord Rees from 1137 to 1197. The age was, in many respects, a great one.

It was, of course, an age of war. Up to 1154, during the reign of Stephen, the English barons were fighting against each other, and the king had very little power over them. The most important Norman barons in Wales were the Earls of Chester in the valley of the Dee, the Mortimers on the upper Wye, the Braoses on the upper Usk, and the Clares in the south. Their castles were a continual menace to the country they had so far failed to conquer, and the Lord Rees was glad to get Kidwelly, and Owen Gwynedd to get Mold and Rhuddlan.

It was, on the whole, an age of unity. It was the chief aim of Owen Gwynedd to be the ally of the Lord Rees; and in this he succeeded, though his brother Cadwaladr, in his desire for Ceredigion, had killed Rees' brother, to Owen's infinite sorrow. The princes of Powys, Madoc and Owen Cyveiliog, were in the same alliance also, and they were helped in their struggle with the Normans. Unity was never more necessary. Henry II. brought great armies into Wales. Once he came along the north coast to Rhuddlan. At another time he tried to cross the Berwyn, but was beaten back by great storms. Had he reached the upper Dee, he would have found the united forces of the Lord Rees, Owen Cyveiliog, and Owen Gwynedd at Corwen. There are many stirring episodes in these wars: the fight at Consilt, when Henry II. nearly lost his life; the scattering of his tents on the Berwyn by a storm that seemed to be the fury of fiends; the reckless exposure of life in storming a wall or in the shock of battle. But the Norman brought new cruelty into war: Henry II. took out the eyes of young children because their fathers had revolted against him; and William de Braose invited a great number of Welsh chiefs to a feast in his castle at Abergavenny, and there murdered them all.

It is a relief to turn to another feature of the age: it was an age of great men. Owen Gwynedd was probably the greatest. He disliked war, but he was an able general; he made Henry II. retire without great loss of life to his own army. He was a thoughtful prince, of a loving nature and high ideals, and his court was the home of piety and culture. He is more like our own ideal of a prince than any of the other princes of the Middle Ages. The Lord Rees was not less wise, and his life is less sorrowful and more brilliant. He also was as great as a statesman as he was as a general; and he made his peace with the English king in order to make his country quiet and rich. Owen Cyveiliog was placed in a more difficult position than either of his allies; he was nearer to very ambitious Norman barons. He was great as a warrior; often had his white steed been seen leading the rush of battle. He was greater as a statesman: friend and foe said that Owen was wise; and he was greater still as a poet.

The age was an age of poetry. A generation of great Welsh poets found an equal welcome in the courts of Gwynedd, Powys, and Deheubarth; and even the Norman barons of Morgannwg began to feel the charm of Welsh legend and song; Robert of Gloucester was a great patron of learning. One of the chief events of the period was Lord Rees' great Eisteddvod at Cardigan in 1176.

It was an age of new ideals. The Crusades were preached in Wales; the grave of Christ was held by a cruel unbeliever, and it was the duty of a soldier to rescue it. It appealed to an inborn love of war, and many Welshmen were willing to go. It did good by teaching them that, in fighting, they were not to fight for themselves. It was in Powys that feuds were most bitter. A young warrior told a preacher, who was trying to persuade him to take the cross: "I will not go until, with this lance, I shall have avenged my lord's death." The lance immediately became shivered in his hand. The lance once used for blind feuds was gradually consecrated to the service of ideals—of patriotism or of religion.

The age of Owen Gwynedd and the Lord Rees and Owen Cyveiliog brought a higher ideal still. If the Crusader made war sacred, the monk made labour noble. The chief aim of the monk, it is true, was to save his soul. He thought the world was very bad, as indeed it was; and he thought he could best save his own soul by retiring to some remote spot, to live a life of prayer. But he also lived a life of labour; he became the best gardener, the best farmer, and the best shepherd of the Middle Ages. Great monasteries were built for him, and great tracts of land were given him, by those who were anxious that he should pray for their souls. The monk who came to Wales was the Cistercian. The monasteries of Tintern, Margam, and Neath were built by Norman barons; and Strata Florida, Valle Crucis, and Basingwerk showed that the Welsh princes also welcomed the monks.

Better, then, than the brilliant wars were the poets and the great Eisteddvod. Better still, perhaps, were the orchards and the flocks of the peaceful monks.

CHAPTER X: LLYWELYN THE GREAT

On the death of the Lord Rees, one of the grandsons of Owen Gwynedd becomes the central figure in Welsh history. Llywelyn the Great rose into power in 1194, and reigned until 1240—a long reign, and in many ways the most important of all the reigns of the Welsh princes.

Llywelyn's first task was to become sole ruler in Gwynedd. The sons of Owen Gwynedd had divided the strong Gwynedd left them by their father, and their nobles and priests could not decide which of the sons was to be supreme. Iorwerth, the poet Howel, David, Maelgwn, Rhodri, tried to get Gwynedd, or portions of it. Eventually, David I. became king; but soon a strong opposition placed Llywelyn, the able son of Iorwerth, on the throne. Uncles and cousins showed some jealousy; but the growing power of Llywelyn soon made them obey him with gradually diminishing envy.

His next task was to attach the other princes of Wales to him, now that the Lord Rees and Owen Cyveiliog were dead. To begin with, he had to deal with the astute Gwenwynwyn, the son of Owen Cyveiliog; and he had to be forced to submit. He then turned to the many sons and grandsons of the Lord Rees—Maelgwn and Rees the Hoarse especially. They called John, King of England, into Wales; but they soon found that Llywelyn was a better master than John and his barons. Gradually Llywelyn established a council of chiefs—partly a board of conciliation, and partly an executive body. It was nothing new; but it was a striking picture of the way in which Llywelyn meant to join the princes into one organised political body.

His third task was to begin to unite Norman barons and Welsh chiefs under his own rule. He had to begin in the old way, by using force; and Ranulph of Chester and the Clares trembled for the safety of their castles. He then offered political alliance; and some of the Norman families of the greatest importance in the reign of John—the Earl of Chester, the family of Braose, and the Marshalls of Pembroke—became his allies. His other step was to unite Welsh and Norman families by marriage. He himself married a daughter of King John, and he gave his own daughters in marriage to a Braose and a Mortimer. It is through the dark-haired Gladys, who married Ralph Mortimer, that the kings of England can trace their descent from the House of Cunedda.

Llywelyn's last great task was to make relations between England and Wales relations of peace and amity. During his long reign, he saw three kings on the throne of England—the crusader Richard, the able John, and the worthless and mean Henry III. It was with John that he had most to do, the king whose originality and vices have puzzled and shocked so many historians. John helped him to crush Gwenwynwyn, then helped the jealous Welsh princes to check the growth of his power. Llywelyn saw that it was his policy, as long as John was alive, to join the English barons. They were then trying to force Magna Carta upon the King, that great document which prevented John from interfering with the privileges of his barons. In that document John promises, in three clauses, that he will observe the rights of Welshmen and the law of Wales.

When John died in 1216, and his young son Henry succeeded him, the policy of England was guided by William Marshall Earl of Pembroke. William Marshall was one of the ministers of Henry II., and by his marriage with the daughter of Strongbow, the conqueror of Ireland, he had become Earl of Pembroke. It was with him that Llywelyn had now to deal. He was too strong in Pembroke to be attacked, but his very presence made it easier for Llywelyn to retain the allegiance of the chiefs who would have been in danger from the Norman barons if Llywelyn's protection were taken away. In 1219 the great William Marshall died; and changes in English politics forced his sons into an alliance with Llywelyn.

Llywelyn's title of Great is given him by his Norman and English contemporaries. He was great as a general; his detection of trouble before the storm broke, his instant determination and rapidity of movements, his ever-ready munitions for battle and siege, made his later campaigns always successful. He felt that he was carrying on war in his own country; so his wars were not wars of devastation, but the crushing of armies and the razing of castles.

He took an interest in the three great agents in the civilisation of the time—the bard, the monk, and the friar. The bard was as welcome as ever at his court; the monk, welcomed by Owen Gwynedd before, was given another home at Aber Conway. Llywelyn extended his welcome to the friar, and he was given a home at Llan Vaes in Anglesey, on the shores of the Menai. The friar brought a higher ideal than that of the monk; his aim was salvation, not by prayer in the solitude of a mountain glen, but by service where men were thickest together—even in streets made foul by vice, and haunted by leprosy. Of the Mendicant Orders, the Franciscans were the best known in Wales; and, of all Orders of that day, it was they who sympathised most deeply with the sorrows of men. And it was this which, a little later on, brought them so much into politics.

Great and successful in war and policy, in touch with the noblest influences in the life of the time, Llywelyn applied himself to one last task. His companions and allies had nearly all died before him; but he wished that the peace and unity, which they had established, should live after them. He had two sons—Griffith, who was the champion of independence; and David, who wished for peace with England. Llywelyn laid more stress on strong government at home than on the repudiation of feudal allegiance to the King of England. So he persuaded the council of princes at Strata Florida to accept David as his successor.

CHAPTER XI: THE LAST LLYWELYN

David II, a mild and well-meaning prince, was too weak to carry his father's policy out. He tried to maintain peace, and did homage to his uncle, the King of England. But, as the head of the patriotic party, his more energetic brother, Griffith, opposed him. By guile he caught Griffith, and shut him in a castle on the rock of Criccieth. The other princes shook off the yoke of Gwynedd, and Henry III tried to play the brothers against each other. David sent Griffith to Henry, who put him in the Tower of London. In trying to escape, his rope broke, and he fell to the ground dead. Soon afterwards, in 1246, in the middle of a war with Henry, David died of a broken heart.

The sons of Griffith—Owen, Llywelyn, and David—at once took their uncle's place; and by 1255 Llywelyn ap Griffith was sole ruler. By that year Henry III had given his young son Edward the earldom of Chester, which had fallen to the crown, and the lands between the Dee and the Conway, which he claimed by a treaty with the dead Griffith. Thus Edward and Llywelyn began their long struggle.

Between 1255 and 1267 Llywelyn tries to recover his grandfather's position in Wales. In 1255 his power extended over Gwynedd only. He found it easy to extend it over most of Wales, because the rule of the English officials made the Welsh chiefs long for the protection of Gwynedd. The Barons' War paralysed the power of the King, and Llywelyn made an alliance with Simon de Montfort and the barons. Even after Montfort's fall in 1265 the barons were so powerful that the King was still at their mercy. In 1267 Llywelyn's position as Prince of Wales was recognised in the Treaty of Montgomery. His sway extended from Snowdon to the Dee on the east, and to the Teivy and the Beacons on the south—practically the whole of modern Wales, except the southern seaboard. Within these wide bounds all the Welsh barons were to swear fealty to Llywelyn, the only exception being Meredith ap Rees of Deheubarth.

The second struggle of Llywelyn's reign took place between 1267 and 1277. He tried to weld his land into a closer union, and many of the chiefs of the south and east became willing to call in the English King. Two of them, his own brother David and Griffith of Powys, fled to England, and were received by Edward, who had been king since 1272. Llywelyn and Edward distrusted each other. Edward wished to unite Britain in a feudal unity, and to crush all opponents. Llywelyn thought of helping the barons; he might become their leader. Eleanor, the daughter of Simon de Montfort, the old leader of the barons, was betrothed to him. War broke out. The barons—Clares and Mortimers, and all—joined the King. Llywelyn's dominions were invaded at all points, his barons had to yield, one after the other; and finally, in 1277, Llywelyn had to accept the Treaty of Rhuddlan. His dominions shrunk to the old limits of Snowdon, his sway over the rest of Wales was taken from him, and the title of Prince of Wales was to cease with his life.

The third struggle was between 1277 and 1282. The rule of the new officials drove the Welsh to revolt; and the chiefs who had opposed Llywelyn, especially his brother David, begged for Llywelyn's protection. Eleanor, Llywelyn's wife and Edward's cousin, tried to keep the peace, but she died while they were arming for the last bitter war of 1282.

It was comparatively easy for Edward to overrun Powys or Deheubarth, if he had an army strong enough. But at that time Gwynedd was almost impregnable. From Conway to Harlech lies the vast mass of Snowdon, a great natural rampart running from sea to sea. Its steep side is towards the east, and the invader found before him heights which he could not climb, and round which he could not pass. If you stand in the Vale of Conway, look at the hills on the Arvon side—the great natural wall of inmost Gwynedd, with its last tower, the Penmaen Mawr, rising right from the sea. The gentle slopes are to the west, and there the corn and flocks were safe.

Edward had to put a large army into the field, and it cost him much. In the war with Llywelyn he had to change the English army entirely; and, in order to get money, he had to allow the Parliament to get life and power. To carry supplies, and to land men in Anglesey to turn the flank of the Welsh, he wanted a fleet. But there was no royal navy then, and the fishermen of the east coast and the south coast—who had no quarrel with the Welsh, but were very anxious to fight each other—were not willing to lose their fish harvest in order to fight so far away.

In 1282, Edward's great army closed round Snowdon. The chiefs still faithful to Llywelyn had to yield or flee. But winter was coming on, and could Edward keep his army in the field? An attempt had been made to enter Snowdon from Anglesey, but the English force was destroyed at Moel y Don. It looked as if Edward would have to retire. Llywelyn left Snowdon, and went to Ceredigion and the Vale of Towy to put new heart in his allies, and from there he passed on to the valley of the Wye. He meant, without a doubt, to get the barons of the border, Welsh and English, to unite against Edward. But in some chance skirmish a soldier slew him, not knowing who he was. When they heard that their Prince was fallen, his men in Snowdon entirely lost heart. They had no faith in David, and in a few months the whole of Wales was at Edward's feet.

CHAPTER XII: CONQUERED WALES

The war between Edward and Llywelyn was not a war between England and Wales, as we think of these countries now. Some of the best soldiers under Edward were Welsh, especially the bowmen who followed the Earl of Gloucester and Roger Mortimer from the Wye and Severn valleys.

It is not right that we Welshmen should feel bitter against England, because, in this last war, Edward won and Llywelyn fell. It is easy to say that Edward was cruel and faithless, and it is easy to say that Llywelyn was shifty and obstinate; but it is quite clear that each of them thought that he was right. Edward thought that Britain ought to be united: Llywelyn thought Wales ought to be free. Now, happily, we have the union and the freedom.

On the other hand, I should not like you to think that Wales was more barbarous than England, or Llywelyn less civilised than Edward I. Giraldus Cambrensis saw a prince going barefoot, and the fussy little Archbishop Peckham saw that Welsh marriage customs were not what he liked; and many historians, who have never read a line of Welsh poetry, take for granted that the conquest of Wales was a new victory for civilisation.

In many ways Wales was more civilised than England at that time. Its law was more simple and less developed, it is true; but it was more just in many cases, and certainly more humane. Was it not better that the land should belong to the people, and that the youngest son should have the same chance as the eldest? And, in crime, was it not better that if no opportunity for atonement was given, the death of the criminal was to be a merciful one? In the reign of John, a Welsh hostage, a little boy of seven, was hanged at Shrewsbury, because his father, a South Wales chief, had rebelled. In the reign of Edward I., the miserable David was dragged at the tails of horses through the streets of the same town, and the tortures inflicted on the dying man were too horrible to describe to modern ears. And what the Norman baron did, his Welsh tenant learnt to do. In Wales you get fierce frays and frequent shedding of blood; on the borders you get callous cruelty to a prisoner, or the disfiguring of dead bodies—even that of Simon de Montfort, the greatest statesman of the Middle Ages in England—on the battlefield when all passion was spent.

Take the rulers of Wales again. Griffith ap Conan and Llywelyn the Great had the energy and the foresight, though their sphere was so much smaller, of Henry II. And what English king, except Alfred, attracts one on account of lovableness of character as Owen Gwynedd and Owen Cyveiliog and the Lord Rees do?

When Edward entered into Snowdon, Welsh was spoken to the Dee and the Severn, and far beyond. There were many dialects, as there are still, though any two Welshmen could understand each other wherever they came from, with a little patience, as they can still. But there was also a literary language, and this was understood, if not spoken, by the chiefs all through the country. It was more like the Welsh spoken in mid-Wales—especially in the valley of the Dovey—than any other. There are many signs of civilisation; one of them is the possession of a literary language—for romance and poem, for court and Eisteddvod.

Conquered Wales may be divided into two parts—the Wales conquered by the Norman barons and the Wales conquered by the English king.

The Wales conquered by the English king was the country ruled by Llywelyn and his allies. In 1284, by the statute of Rhuddlan, it was formed into six shires. The Snowdon district—which held out last—was made into the three shires of Anglesey, Carnarvon, and Merioneth. The part of the land between Conway and Dee that belonged to the king, not to barons, was made into the shire of Flint. The lands of Llywelyn's allies beyond the Dovey were made into the shires of Cardigan and Carmarthen. Instead of the chiefs of the Welsh prince, the king's sheriffs and justices ruled the country. But much of the old law remained.

The Wales conquered by the Norman barons lay to the east and south of the Wales turned into shires in 1284. It included the greater part of the valleys of the Clwyd, Dee, Severn, and Wye; and the South Wales coast from Gloucester to Pembroke. It remained in the possession of lords who were subject to the King of England, but who ruled almost like kings in their own lordships. The laws and customs of the various lordships differed greatly; sometimes the lord used English law, and sometimes Welsh law. The great ruling families changed much in wealth and power, from century to century. In Llywelyn's time the most important were the Clares (Gloucester and Glamorgan), the Mortimers (Wigmore and Chirk), Lacy (Denbigh), Warenne (Bromfield and Yale), Fitzalan (Oswestry), Bohun (Brecon), Braose (Gower), and Valence (Pembroke).

Llywelyn was the last prince of independent Wales. From that time on, the title is conferred by the King of England on his eldest son, who is then crowned. The present Prince of Wales also comes, through a daughter of Llywelyn the Great, from the House of Cunedda, the princes of which ruled Wales from Roman times to 1284. Of all the houses that have gone to make the royal house, this is the most ancient.

CHAPTER XIII: CASTLE AND LONG-BOW

So far I have told you very little about war, except that a battle was fought and lost, or a castle built or taken.

War has two sides—attack and defence. New ways of attacking and defending are continually devised. When the art of defence is more perfect than the art of attack, the world changes very little, for the strong can keep what he has gained. When the art of attack is the more perfect, new men have a better chance, and many changes are made. The chief source of defence was the castle, the chief weapon of attack was the long-bow. Wales contains the most perfect castles in this country; it is also the home of the long-bow. From 1066 to 1284 England and Wales were conquered, and the conquest was permanent because castles were built. From 1284 to 1461, England and Wales attacked other countries, and the weapon which gave them so many victories was the long-bow.

I will tell you about the castles first, about the Norman castles and about the Edwardian castles.

The Norman castle was a square keep, with walls of immense thickness, sometimes of 20 feet. But if the Norman had to build on the top of a hill or on the ruins of an old castle, he did not try to make the new castle square, but allowed its walls to take the form of the hill or of the old castle; and this kind of castle was called a shell keep. The outer and inner casing of the wall would be of dressed stone, the middle part was chiefly rubble. At first, if they had plenty of supplies, a very few men could hold a castle against an army as long as they liked. These were the castles built by the Norman invaders to retain their hold over the Welsh districts they conquered.

But many ways of storming a castle were discovered. They could be scaled by means of tall ladders, especially in a stealthy night attack. Stones could be thrown over the walls by mangonels to annoy the garrison. Sometimes a wall could be brought down by a battering-ram. But the quickest and surest way was by mining. The miners worked their way to the wall, and then began to take some of the stones of the outer casing out, propping the wall up with beams of wood. When the hole was big enough, they filled it with firewood; they greased the beams well, they set fire to them and then retired to a safe distance to see what happened. When the great wall crashed down, the soldiers swarmed over it to beat down the resistance of the garrison. If ever you go to Abergavenny Castle, in the Vale of Usk, look at the cleft in the rock along which the daring besiegers once climbed. And if you go to the Vale of Towy, and see Dryslwyn Castle, remember that the wall once came down before the miners expected, and that many men were crushed.

In order to prevent mining, many changes were made. Moats were dug round the castle, and filled with water. Brattices were made along the top of the towers, galleries through the floor of which the defenders could pour boiling pitch on the besiegers. The walls were built at such angles that a window, with archers posted behind it, could command each wall. Stronger towers were built—round towers with a coping at each storey, solid as a rock, which would crack and lean without falling; there is a leaning tower at Caerphilly Castle. One other way I must mention—the child or the wife of the castellan would be brought before the walls, and hanged before his eyes unless he opened the gates.

The newer or Edwardian castles, those of the reigns of Henry III. and Edward I., are concentric—that is, there are several castles in one; so that the besiegers, when they had taken one castle, found themselves face to face with another, still stronger, perhaps, inside it. Of these castles, the most elaborate is the castle of Caerphilly, built by Gilbert de Clare, the Red Earl of Gloucester who helped Edward in the Welsh wars. And it was by means of these magnificent concentric castles—Conway, Beaumaris, Carnarvon, and Harlech—that Edward hoped to keep Wales.

There are many kinds of bows. In war two were used—the cross-bow and the long-bow. The cross-bow was meant at first for the defence of towns, like Genoa or the towns of Castile. So strength was more important than lightness, and the archer had time to take aim. It was a bow on a cross piece of wood, along which the string was drawn back peg after peg by mechanism. The bow was then held to the breast, and the arrow let off. It was clumsy, heavy, and expensive.

The long-bow was only one piece of sinewy yew, and a string. It was used at first for the chase, and the archer had to take instant aim. It was drawn to the ear, and it was a most deadly weapon when a strong arm had been trained to draw it. Its arrow could pick off a soldier at the top of the highest castle; it could pierce through an oak door three fingers thick; it could pin a mail-clad knight to his horse. It was this peasant weapon that brought the mailed knight down in battle.

The home of the long-bow is the country between the Severn and the Wye. It was famous before, but it was first used with effect in the last Welsh wars. It was used to break the lines of the Snowdon lances and pikes, so that the mail-clad cavalry might dash in. But later on, the same bows were used to bring the nobles of France down.

From the Welsh war on, archers and infantry became important; battles ceased to be what they had been so long—the shock of mail-clad knights meeting each other at full charge.

The long-bow made noble and peasant equal on the field of battle. The revolution was made complete later on by gunpowder.

CHAPTER XIV: THE RISE OF THE PEASANT

I have told you much about princes and soldiers, but very little about the lowly life of peasants, and the trade of towns.

The conquest of Wales, by Norman baron and English king, tended to raise the serf to the level of the freeman. The chief causes of the rise of the serf were the following:

1 The ignorance of the English officials. The Norman baron very often paid close attention to the privileges of the classes he ruled, and the Welsh freeman retained his superiority. But the English officials—and Edward II. found that they were far too numerous in Wales—often refused to distinguish between a Welshman who was an innate freeman and a Welshman who lived on a serf maenol. Their aim was to make them all pay the same tax.

2. The fall in the value of money. At the time of the Norman Conquest, silver coins were rare, and their value high. But, in exchange for cloth and wool, of arrows and spears, of mountain ponies and cattle, coins came in great numbers, and it was easier for the serf to earn them. That is the value of coins became less.

This was a great boon to all who were bound to pay fixed sums—the freeman who paid to the king the dues he used to pay to his prince, the serf who paid to his lord a sum of money instead of service. All ancient servitude, political and economic, was commuted for money; as the money became easier to get, the serf became the more free.

3. The rise of towns and the growth of commerce. We must not, however, think of commerce as if it had been first brought by the Normans. There had been roads and coins in Roman times. The Danes had been traders, probably, before they became pirates and invaders. Timber, millstones, cattle, coarse cloth, and arrow-heads crossed the Severn eastwards before the Normans saw it; and corn was carried westward. There were close relations, political and commercial, between Wales and Ireland from very early times.

But the Norman and English Conquests revived and quickened trade. Towns rose, regular markets were established, and the barons who took tolls protected the merchants who paid them. Every baron had a castle, every castle needed a walled town, and a town cannot live except by trade. In the town the baron did not ask a Welshman whether he had been free or serf; the townsmen were strangers, and they welcomed the serf who came to work.

4. The monk and the friar. The bard was a freeman born, a skilled weaver of courteous phrases, not a churlish taeog. The monk or friar might be a serf. They worked like serfs, and ennobled labour. The Church condemned serfdom, and we find chapters giving their serfs freedom.

5. The Scotch and French wars of the English kings gave employment to hosts of bowmen and of men-at-arms, and to the numerous attendants required to look after the horses by means of which the army moved. The greater use of infantry after the reign of Edward I. caused a greater demand for the peasant; and the use of the cheap long-bow gave him a value in war. There were five thousand Welsh archers and spearmen on the field of Cressy. In these and other ways the serf was becoming free.

You would expect a gradual, almost unconscious struggle, between the serf and his lord for political power. The struggle came, but it was conscious and very fierce. It was brought about by a terrible pestilence, known as the Black Death. This plague came slowly and steadily from the East; in 1348 it reached Bristol, and it probably swept away one half of the people of the towns of Wales. It was not the towns alone that it visited; it came to the mountain glens as well. It was a most deadly disease. It killed, for one thing, because people believed that they would die. They saw the dark spots on the skin before they became feverish; they recognised the black mark of the Death and they gave themselves up for lost.

Labourers became very scarce. They claimed higher wages. The lords tried to drag them back into serfdom; they tried to force them by law to take the old wage. On both sides of the Severn the labourers took arms, and waged war against their lords. The peasant war in England is called the Peasant Revolt; the peasant war in Wales is sometimes called the revolt of Owen Glendower.

A change came over the rebellions in Wales. At first, the rebellions were those of Llywelyn's country; the allies who had deserted him, and then turned against Edward, like Rees ap Meredith; or his own followers, like Madoc, who said he was his son; or men he had protected, like Maelgwn Vychan in Pembroke. Later on, under Edward II. and Edward III., the rebellions were against the march lords, and the king was looked upon as a protector—such as the rebellion of Llywelyn Bren against the Clares and Mortimers in Glamorgan in 1316. But the wilder spirits went to the French wars, and fought for both sides. With the assassination of Owen of Wales in 1378, the last of Llywelyn's near relatives to dream of restoring the independence of Wales, the rebellions against the King of England came to an end.

When they broke out again, it was not in Snowdon or Ceredigion; the old dominions of Llywelyn were almost unwilling to rise. The new revolts were in the march lands, and especially in the towns.

CHAPTER XV: OWEN GLENDOWER

The English baron in Wales tried to add to his possessions by encroaching on the lands of the Welsh freemen. His estate always remained the same, because it all went to the eldest son, according to what is called primogeniture; their lands, on the other hand, were divided between the sons according to what is called gavelkind. He also, by laws they did not understand, took the waste land—forest and mountain. As one man can more easily watch his interest than many, the baron succeeded; but the freemen felt that they were being robbed.

The tenants of the barons were restless and rebellious; they said they were free, that they would not work as serfs, that they would not bring food rents, but that they would pay a fixed rent for every acre they held.

At Ruthin, in the Vale of Clwyd, there was a baron called Lord Grey; and in the valley of the Dee there was a Welsh squire called Owen Glendower. Their lands met, and Grey took part of Owen's sheep walk. Owen had been a law student at Westminster, and he had served Henry of Lancaster. In 1399 Richard II. had been dethroned, and the barons had made Henry of Lancaster king as Henry IV. Owen saw, however, that the king was too weak to curb his lawless barons, and in 1400 he attacked Lord Grey, and burnt Ruthin.

The rebellion that had long been smouldering burst into a flame all over the country. Owen was at once welcomed by the bard, the friar, and the peasant. The bard hailed his star as that of the heir of the princes, who had come to deliver his country. The friar welcomed him as the friend of the poor and of learning; and unruly students from Oxford, then the centre of a great intellectual awakening, flocked home to march under his banner. The peasant welcomed him as his protector against the steward of his lord. The main strength of the movement was the peasant revolt; and Welsh poets, like the English ones, sang the praises of the ploughman and of the plough.

Owen's success was most rapid, so rapid that it was put down to magic. In four years the whole of Wales recognised him as its prince. Henry IV. and Prince Henry came to Wales, made rapid marches and retook castles, punished the friars of Llan Vaes and the monks of Strata Florida. But their victories led to nothing, and the storms fought against them. Owen's victories were used to the full—that of the Vyrnwy was followed by an agreement with Grey of Ruthin, that of Bryn Glas by an alliance with the Mortimers. His marches were nearly all triumphant; he was welcomed along the whole line of the marches by the peasants to the furthest corners of Gwent.

Owen tried to establish a government that the King of England could not overthrow. He had three institutions in mind—an independent Wales, governed by him as Prince in a Parliament of representatives of the commotes; an independent Welsh Church, with an Archbishop of St David's at its head; and an independent system of learning and civilisation, guided by two Universities, one in North Wales and one in South Wales.

The new Wales was to be safeguarded by four alliances—with the English barons, with the Pope, with Scotland, and with France. He failed to save the Percies from their defeat at Shrewsbury in 1403; but he based all his plans on an alliance with the Mortimers, the enemies of Lancaster and the Percies. The head of the Mortimer family had died in Ireland in 1398, and had left four young children. They were the real heirs to the crown, and Owen meant to win their throne for them. Their uncle, Edmund Mortimer, married Glendower's daughter. But the young Earl of March, the elder of the Mortimer boys, had no ambition, and a plot to bring him and his brother to Owen failed.

Owen's alliance with Peter de Luna, the anti-Pope Benedict XIII., gave a certain amount of prestige to his title. The alliance with Scotland, based on common kinship, could bring him no help at that time: because it was torn between two factions during the reign of the weak Robert III.; and the next king, the poet James I., was captured at sea and put into an English prison.

The French alliance was much more promising; it would give what Owen wanted most—siege engines, a fleet, and an army of trained soldiers. Charles VI. of France, the father-in-law of the deposed Richard, refused to make peace with the usurper Henry; his fleet protected the Welsh coast, and in 1405 a French army of 2,800 men landed at Milford.

Owen struggled on, with waning power, until his death in 1415. He came too soon for success, while the power of the House of Lancaster was increasing.

Of all figures in the history of Wales, that of Owen Glendower is the most striking and the most popular. The place of his grave is unknown, his lineage and the date of his death a matter of conjecture; there is much mystery about even his most brilliant years. But his majestic figure, his wisdom, and his ideals remained in the memory of his country. His ghost wandered, it was said, around Valle Crucis. His spirit, more than that of any hero of the past, seems to follow his people on their onward march. This is not on account of his political ideals, but because he was the champion of the peasant and of education.

CHAPTER XVI: THE WARS OF THE ROSES

The reign of Henry V was a reign of brilliant victories in France, and the reign of Henry VI one of disastrous defeats. During both reigns the lords were becoming more powerful in Wales as well as in England. The hold of the king over them became weaker every year; they packed the Parliament, they appointed the Council, they overawed the law courts. If a man wanted security, he must wear the badge of some lord, and fight for him when called upon to do so. In the marches of Wales there were more than a hundred lords holding castle and court; and it was easy for a robber or a murderer to escape from one lordship to the other, or even to find a welcome and protection. In Wales and in the marches the lords preyed upon their weaker neighbours, and the country became full of private war.

The selfish families, all fighting for more land and more power, gradually formed themselves into two parties—the parties of the Red Rose and of the White Rose. The leading family in the Red Rose party was that of Lancaster, represented by the saintly King Henry VI.; the leading family in the White Rose party was that of York. In the Wars of the Roses, York and Lancaster fought over the crown, and those who supported them over a castle or an estate.

Wales was divided. The west was for Lancaster, from Pembroke to Harlech, and from Harlech to Anglesey. The east was for York, from Cardiff and Raglan to Wigmore, and from Wigmore to Chirk. Lancaster held estates in Wales and on the border—the castles of Hereford, Skenfrith, Ogmore, and Kidwelly being centres of strength and wealth. York's chief country was the march of Wales, with Ludlow as its centre. The Welsh barons took sides according to their interests. Jasper Tudor, Earl of Pembroke, held the west for his half-brother, the king. Sir William Herbert, who was very powerful in the country south of the Mortimers, took the side of his powerful neighbour. Others wavered, especially Grey of Ruthin and the Stanleys in North Wales.

One battle was fought between the Welsh Yorkists and the Welsh Lancastrians. This was the battle of Mortimer's Cross, near Wigmore, in February 1461. The victor was the young Duke of York, who was crowned king as Edward IV later in the year. An old man, Owen Tudor, the father of Jasper Tudor, and the grandfather of the boy who was "to rule after them all" as Henry VII., was taken prisoner. They took him to Hereford, and there they cut his head off and set it on the market cross. The battles of the Wars of the Roses were very cruel ones; the noble prisoners that had been taken, even children of tender age, were murdered in cold blood on the evening of the battle. "By God's blood," said one, as he killed a child, "thy father slew mine, and so will I do thee."

The Welsh barons led their men to nearly all the important battles. North Wales archers, wearing the three feathers of the Prince of Wales, fought for Lancaster in the snow at the great defeat of Towton on the Palm Sunday of 1461; the archers of Gwent, led by Herbert, fought vainly for York at the battle of Edgecote, in the summer of 1469. And the Welsh waverer and traitor was seen in battle also—Grey of Ruthin led the van for Lancaster at the battle of Northampton in 1460, and caused the battle to be lost by deserting to York at the be ginning of the fighting. In Wales itself, also, the war was fought bitterly; and the stubborn defence of Harlech for the Lancastrians became famous through the whole country. The last battle fought between Lancaster and York was the battle of Tewkesbury, in May 1471, and Lancaster lost it; the Prince of Wales, the king's only son, was killed; and his heroic mother, Margaret of Anjou, gave the struggle up. A young Welsh noble—Henry Tudor, Earl of Richmond—became the Lancastrian heir. The fortunes of his house were hopeless, however; and his uncle, Jasper, sent him in safety to Brittany.

The Yorkist kings, Edward IV. and Richard III., in spite of cruelty and murder, ruled well. They broke the power of the barons, and they made the people rich—by maintaining peace, by repressing piracy, by protecting the woollen industry of the towns.

In Wales their rule was for peace and order. They made a Court for Wales at Ludlow, the home of their race. From Ludlow they began to force the barons to do justice and to obey the king. It seemed as if the rule of the Yorkists was to be a long one, for they were very popular in London and the towns.

But the nobles were not willing to see their power taken from them day by day. Jasper Tudor appealed to the loyalty of the Welsh, and the men of West Wales wanted a king of their own blood; for the laws had been made unjust to them ever since the time of Owen Glendower.

Many attempts were made, and they failed. But at last, on August 7, 1485, the fugitive Earl of Richmond came to Milford Haven. He marched on to the valley of the Teivy, and he was joined by Sir Rees ap Thomas, and an army of South Wales men; he journeyed on through the valley of the Severn, and the North Wales men joined him; English nobles joined him as he marched by Shrewsbury, Stafford, Lichfield, and Tamworth. Richard's army was also on the march. At Bosworth, August 22, 1485, the two armies met in the last battle of the Wars of the Roses. Richard fought fiercely, wearing his crown; and when he was defeated and killed, the crown was placed on Henry's head.

The people of England did not care who ruled, Richard or Henry, as long as he kept order, for they were very tired of civil war. But the people of Wales welcomed Henry as a Welshman who would rule them kindly and justly.

CHAPTER XVII: TUDOR ORDER

The Tudors—Henry VII., his son, Henry VIII., and his three grandchildren, Edward VI. and Mary and Elizabeth—ruled England and Wales from 1485 to 1603. Under them the people became united, law-abiding, patriotic, and prosperous. The Tudor period is justly regarded as the most glorious in British history, with its great statesmen, its great adventurers, and its great poets.

The Tudors were loyally supported by Wales, by the military strength of men like Sir Rees ap Thomas or the Earl of Pembroke, and by the diplomatic skill of the Cecils. Under their rule—hard and unmerciful, but just and efficient—the law became strong enough to crush the mightiest and to shield the weakest. Welshmen found that, even under their own sovereigns, their ancient language was regarded as a hindrance and their patriotism as a possible source of trouble; but they obtained the privileges of an equal race, and they were pleased to regard themselves as a dominant one.

They obtained equal political privileges. The laws which denied them residence in the garrison towns in Wales, or the holding of land in England, came to an end. The whole of the country, shire ground and march ground, was divided into one system of shires and given representation in Parliament, by the Act of Union of 1535. It is called an Act of Union because, by it, Wales and England were united on equal terms.

Anglesey, Carnarvon, Merioneth, Flint, Cardigan, and Carmarthen had been shires since I 284; and small portions of Glamorgan and Pembroke had been governed like shires, so that some Tudor writers call them counties. The chief difference between a shire and a lordship is that the king's writ runs to the shire, but not to the lordship. The king administers the law in the shire, through the sheriff; the lord administers the law in the lordship through his own officials.

In 1535 the marches of Wales were turned into shire ground. The bulk of them went to make seven new shires—Pembroke, Glamorgan, Monmouth, Brecon, Radnor, Montgomery, and Denbigh. The others were added to the older English and Welsh counties. Of these, those added to Shropshire and Herefordshire and Gloucestershire became part of England. Monmouth also was declared to be an English shire, for judicial purposes; but it has remained sturdily Welsh, and now it is practically regarded by Parliament as part of Wales. The whole country was now governed in the same way, and

Wales was represented, like England, in Parliament. No attempt had been made to do this before, except by the first English Prince of Wales, the weak and unfortunate Edward II.

Of even greater value than political equality was the new reign of law. The Tudors used the Star Chamber, the Court of Wales, and the Great Sessions of Wales, to make all equal before the law. To the Star Chamber they summoned a noble who was still too powerful for the court of law.

But it was the Court of Wales that did most work. It was held at Ludlow. It had very able presidents, men like Bishop Lee, the Earl of Pembroke, and Sir Henry Sidney. Bishop Lee struck terror into the whole Welsh march, between 1534 and 1543. Before his time a lord would keep murderers and robbers at his castle, protect them, and perhaps share their spoil. But no man could keep a felon out of the reach of Bishop Rowland Lee. If he could not get them alive he got their dead bodies; and you might have seen processions of men carrying sacks on ponies—they were dead men who were to swing on Ludlow gibbets. But, severe as Lee was, the peasant was glad that he could go to the Court at Ludlow instead of going to the court of a march lord, as he had to do before 1535. The shire had been much better governed than the lordship. When the lordship of Mawddwy was added to the shire of Merioneth in 1535, the officers of the shire found that it was a nest of brigands and outlaws.

In the more peaceful and humane days of Queen Elizabeth, Sir Henry Sidney became President of the Court of Wales. He was one of the best men of the day; and he was proud of ruling Wales and the border counties, "a third part of this realm," because his high office made him able "to do good every day."

Besides the Court of Wales for the whole country, a court of justice was held in each of four groups of shires; and these courts were called the Great Sessions of Wales. So, though the law was the same for everybody, Wales had a separate system to itself, partly because there was so much to do, and partly because the central courts in London were so far away. Much was also done to get wise and learned justices of the peace, and fair juries.

By the end of the reign of Elizabeth, the last of the Tudors, one may say that Wales rejoiced in the following:

1. There was no hatred between England and Wales; the Welsh gentry served the Queen on land and sea, and the people were more happy and contented than they had been since the time of Llywelyn.

2. There was no danger of private war between lords, to which the peasant might be summoned. The brigands which infested parts of the country had been cleared away.

3. The law of land had been fixed. It was determined that land was to go to the eldest son, according to the English fashion. All the land became the property of some landlord, and it was decided who was a landowner, and who was not. The Welsh freemen were held to own their land; the Welsh serfs, the descendants of an old conquered race, sometimes became owners and sometimes tenants. They all thought that Henry VII., the Welsh victor of Bosworth, had set them free.

4. The Tudors trusted their people, and called upon them to govern and to administer justice themselves. The squires were to be justices, the freemen were to be jurors; the shire was to look after the militia, and the parish after the poor.

CHAPTER XVIII: THE REFORMATION

The Reformation in England was, to begin with, a purely political movement. Henry VIII. wished to rule his people in his own way, in religion as well as in politics; and, eventually, he became Supreme Head of the Church as well as the king of the country. His new power brought changes. It was necessary to reform the Church, and the wealth of the monasteries tempted him to do it. There was a new spirit of enquiry, and the King was led on by that spirit, with dilatory and hesitating steps, to examine old creeds. The religious fervour of the Reformation had caught the people; and the King stood still, if he did not turn back.

But his ministers had no misgivings. Thomas Cromwell tried to hurry the Reformation on—the monasteries were dissolved, the Bible was translated, and the sway of Rome was disowned. The king appointed the bishops, decided church cases, and even determined what the creed of his country was to be. Somerset, in the reign of Edward VI., made the movement a doctrinal one, and forced it on with equal vigour.

Wales looked on, with indifference and apathy at first, and then with murmurs. The movement had no attraction: it had many causes of offence. In England the political movement became a patriotic, an intellectual, and a religious movement; and it succeeded. In Ireland, also, it was political, but it could not appeal to patriotism, because it was an English movement; and it failed. In Wales, it was neither welcomed nor opposed; it was simply tolerated, and with a bad grace.

For one thing, it brought English instead of Latin into public worship. Latin, the old language of prayer and even of sermon, was venerated, though not understood. But English was not only not understood, it was also regarded as inferior to Welsh. The Tudors' dislike of various tongues was as strong as their dislike of various jurisdictions. Henry VIII., in giving Welshmen the Act of 1535, says that the tongue of Owen Tudor is "nothing like ne consonant to the natural mother-tongue used within this realm," and enacts that all officials in Wales shall speak English. And, in the same spirit, the Welshman was told that the Kingdom of Heaven was now open to him, but that he must seek it in English, or not at all.

Again, the reformers—men of the type of Bishop Barlow—despised and shocked a people they never understood. The sanctity of St David's, the theme of the best poets of the Middle Ages and the goal of generations of pilgrims, was described by its Protestant bishop—who unroofed the palace in order to get the lead—as a desolate angle frequented only by vagabond pilgrims. A Welshman is not appealed to by what is an insult to his country and a shock to his religion at the same time. The relics were ruthlessly swept away; they were taken possession of by the agents of Cromwell and destroyed, or sent to London. The images carried in the village processions were lost—the images that could keep the superstitious Welshman from hell, or even bring him back from it, or heal his diseases, or keep his cattle from the murrain, and his crops from blight. I only know of one of those relics that can still be seen. It is the healing cup of Nant Eos, a mere fragment of wood. The people's faith in the relics can be estimated from the fact that the cup has been used within the last century.

Again, the monasteries were dissolved. The wealth of the monasteries, their meadows and barns and sheep-runs and fish ponds, were coveted by the rich; the poor thought of them as sources of alms. The monks were good landlords; and they gave freely, not only the comforts of religion, but of their medicinal herbs and stores of food. The Welsh monasteries were not so rich as those of England, and they were all dissolved among the lesser monasteries—those with an income under £200 a year. But though none of them were very rich, they nearly all had almost £200 a year. Their loss affected the whole country, as each part of Wales had one or two of them—Tintern, Margam, Neath, and Whitland in the south; Strata Florida, Cwm Hir, Ystrad Marchell, and the Vanner in central Wales; and Basingwerk and Maenan in the north.

The Reformation brought the poorer classes in Wales, not only insults to their national and religious feelings, but material loss. It appealed only to the English bishops who had adopted the new Protestant tenets, and to the Welsh and English landowners who had lost their reverence for relics, and had learnt to hunger for land.

The movement was a severe strain on the loyalty of the Welshman to the Tudors, but he had learnt to look to the king for guidances and he suffered in silence. Mary was welcomed, and no Welsh blood was shed for the Protestant faith. The passive resistance to the Reformation might have broken out into a rebellion if a leader had come.

In Elizabeth's reign two attempts were made to disturb the religious settlement. One was made by the Jesuits—the wonderful society established to check the Reformation movement and to lead a reaction against it. In 1583 John Bennett came to North Wales; in 1595 Robert Jones came to Raglan; and several Welsh Jesuits suffered martyrdom. The other attempt was that of John Penry, who wished to appeal to the intellect of the people by means of the pulpit and the printing press. The apostle of the new creed was crushed, like those who wished to revive the old; he was put to death as a traitor in 1593, after a short life of importunate pleading that he might preach the Gospel in Wales.

Before the end of the reign of Elizabeth, however, the Welsh language was recognised. The last school founded, that of Ruthin in 1595, was to have a master who could teach and preach in Welsh. And in 1588 there had appeared, by the help of Archbishop Whitgift, the Welsh Bible of William Morgan. It was the appearance of this Bible that aroused the first real welcome to the Reformation. But the Reformation that gave England a Spenser and a Shakespeare aroused no new life in Wales, not a single hymn or a single prayer.

CHAPTER XIX: THE CIVIL WAR

After the Tudors came the Stuarts. The Tudors did what their people wanted; the king and the people, between them, crushed the nobles. The Stuarts did what they thought right, and they did not try to please the people. Under the Tudors, there was harmony between Crown and Parliament; and Elizabeth left a prosperous people with strong views about their rights and their religion. But James I., and especially his son Charles I., tried to change law and religion. From the Tudor period of unity, then, we come to the Stuart period of strife.

From 1603 to 1642 the struggle went on in Parliament. The Welsh Members nearly all supported the king, and the Welsh people followed the Welsh gentry in strong loyalty. The most famous Welshman of the period was John Williams, who became Archbishop of York and Lord Keeper. He was a wise man; he saw that both sides were a little in the wrong; and if any one could have kept the peace between them, he could have done it. But the king did not quite trust him, and the Parliament almost despised him.

From 1642 to 1646, the First Civil War was waged. This was a war between the king and the Parliament over taxation, militia, and religion. The south-east, and London especially, were for Parliament; the wilder parts, especially Wales, were for the king. The only important part of Wales that declared for Parliament was the southern part of Pembrokeshire, which had been English ever since the reign of Henry II.

Wales was important to the king for two reasons. For one thing, it could give him an army, and he came, time after time, to get a new one. When he unfurled his flag and began the war at Nottingham in 1642, he came to Shrewsbury, and there five thousand Welshmen joined him. With these and others he marched against London, fighting the battle of Edgehill on the way. While the king made many attempts to get London until 1644, and while the New Model army attacked him between 1645 and 1647, the Welsh fought in nearly all his battles, their infantry suffering heavily in the two greatest battles, Marston Moor and Naseby. The war went on in Wales itself also—Rupert and Gerard being the chief Royalist leaders, and Middleton and Michael Jones being the chief Parliamentary ones. No great battles were fought, but there were several skirmishes, and much taking and retaking of castles and towns.

Wales was important to the king, also, because it commanded the two ways to Ireland. The King thought, almost to the last, that an Irish army would save him. Welsh garrisons held the two ports for Ireland, Chester and Bristol. Bristol was stormed by a great midnight assault, and Chester was forced to yield. In March 1647 Harlech yielded, and the war came to an end. By that time the king was a prisoner in the hands of the army.

The Second Civil War, in 1648 and 1649, was a struggle between the two sections of the victorious army. The Parliament wished to establish one religion, the army said that every man must be allowed to worship God as he liked. One was called the Presbyterian ideal, the other the Independent. The army was led by Cromwell, and Parliament was overawed. Then the Presbyterian parts rose in revolt—Kent, Pembrokeshire, and the lowlands of Scotland. The New Model army marched against the Welsh, in order to break the connection between the northern and southern Presbyterians. The Welsh generals were Laugharne, Poyer, and Powell, who had all fought for Parliament in the first war. They were defeated at St Fagans, near Cardiff, and then driven into Pembroke. They determined to hold out to the last within its walls. Cromwell besieged them, and the great feature of the war was the siege of Pembroke. Walls and castles like those of Pembroke had become useless because of gunpowder. But Cromwell could not at once bring his guns so far. His difficulties were increasing daily: the Parliament was trying to come to terms with the king, all Wales around him was disaffected, the Scotch had crossed the border and were marching on London. After many weeks of assaults and desperate defence, the guns came and the old walls were battered down. Pembroke Castle, whose great round tower still stands, had protected William Marshall against Llywelyn and had enabled an important district to remain a "little England beyond Wales," was the last mediæval castle to take an important part in war. The Scotch were soon defeated at the battle of Preston, and the king was brought to trial and put to death, the death-warrant being signed by two Welshmen—John Jones of Merioneth and Thomas Wogan of Cardigan. The date of Charles' execution is January 20, 1649.

The Commonwealth was established immediately, and Wales was looked upon with much distrust—the Presbyterian parts and the Royalist parts—by the new Government. It was represented in the English Parliaments, it is true, but its representatives were often English, and practically appointed by the Government. When the country was put under the military dictatorship of the major-generals, Harrison was sent to rule Wales.

CHAPTER XX: THE GREAT REVOLUTION

Except to the reader who is of a legal or antiquarian turn of mind, the sixteenth and seventeenth centuries are the least interesting in the history of Wales—the very centuries that are the most glorious and the most stirring in the history of England. The older historians stop when they come to the year 1284, and sometimes give a hasty outline of a few rebellions up to 1535. They then give the Welsh a glowing testimonial as a law-abiding and loyal people, and find them too uninteresting to write any more about them.

The history of Wales does, indeed, appear to be nothing more than the gradual disappearance of Welsh institutions. The Court of Wales was restored with the king in 1660; but its work had been done, and it came to an end in 1689. The Great Sessions came to an end in 1830; and, though we now see that their disappearance was a mistake, the bill abolishing them passed through Parliament without a division. The last difference between England and Wales was deleted; and if Wales has no separate existence left, why should we write or read its history?

Because the two centuries of apparent settlement and sleep were the period of a silent revolution, more important, if our aim is to explain the living present rather than the dead past, than all the exciting plots and battles of the House of Cunedda from the rise of Maelgwn to the fall of the last Llywelyn. During these centuries, the history of Wales ceases to be the history of princes and nobles, it becomes the history of the people. Owen Glendower's few years of power were a kind of prophecy; but Owen once appeared to the abbot of Valle Crucis, so tradition says, to declare that he had come before his time. We pass then, very gradually, from the history of a privileged class, speaking literary Welsh, with a literature famous for the wealth of its imagination and the artistic beauty of its form—we pass on to the history of a peasantry, rude and ignorant at first, retaining the servile traits of centuries of subjection, but gradually becoming self-reliant, prosperous, and thoughtful.

The real history of a nation is shown by its literature. Its records and its chronicles are but the notes and comments of various ages. In the period of the princes and nobles, you can trace the rise and decline of a great literature; watch how it gathers strength and beauty from Cynddelw to Dafydd ap Gwilym, and how the strength begins to fail and the beauty to wane, from Dafydd ap Gwilym to Tudur Aled. In the period of the people, from Tudor times on, the peasants tried at first to imitate the poetry of the past; then they began to write and think in their own way. It is not my aim to explain the periods of Welsh literature now; I am going to do that in another book. But, as I have mentioned three typical poets in the period of the princes, I will also mention three poets in the period of the people.

In 1579 Rees Prichard was born; in 1717, Williams Pant y Celyn; in 1832, Islwyn. We have, in these three, writers typical of the seventeenth, eighteenth, and nineteenth centuries respectively. Rees Prichard, still affectionately remembered in every Welsh home as the "Old Vicar," wrote stanzas in the dialect of the Vale of Towy—rough, full of peasant phrases and mangled English words; and he wrote them, not in books, but on the memory of the people. In the same valley, a century later, Williams Pant y Celyn wrote hymns, melodious and inspiring, of great poetic beauty, though with a trace of dialect; they were written and published, but they also haunted every ear that heard them. Beyond the Black Mountains, in the hills of West Monmouth, after another century, Islwyn wrote odes without a trace of dialect; they were written and remained for some time in manuscript; when published, they met with a welcome which shows clearly that Islwyn is the typical poet of modern Welsh thought. If you wish to see and realise the rise of the Welsh peasant, pass from the homely stanzas of the good Old Vicar's Welshmen's Candle to the poetic theology of Pant y Celyn, and from that to the poetic philosophy of Islwyn, where concentrated intensity of thought is expressed in a style that is, at any rate at its best, superior to the best work of the poets of the princes.

If I were to tell you the reasons for this change, I would be writing, in a slightly different form, what I have already written in this book about early Welsh history. The fall of Llywelyn, the Black Death, Owen Glendower's ideals and the Tudor legislation, all prepared the way.

The long-bow and gunpowder, we have seen, made the peasant as important as the noble in war. The long-bow made the coat of mail useless, gunpowder made the castle useless—the defence of the privileges of the Middle Ages departed.

Ideas of equality were advanced. They were looked upon at first as truths applicable only to a perfect and impossible condition, and their discoverers were ignored, if not hanged or burnt. But they always became a reality, and were victorious in the end. Take the truths discovered or championed by Welshmen. Walter Brute rediscovered the theory of justification by faith—that all men are equal in the sight of God, and that no lord could be responsible for them. Bishop Pecock advocated the doctrine of toleration—that reason, not persecution, should rule. John Penry claimed that the people had a right to discuss publicly the questions that vitally affected them. The history of the past shows that the apostles were condemned, the life of the present shows that their ideas lived.

Industry and commerce became more free. In Tudor times piracy was repressed, the march lordships were abolished, the privileges of the towns ceased to fetter manufacture, trade with England became free. In Stuart times roads were made, the industries depending on wool revived, and the industries of Britain began to move westwards towards the iron and the coal. In the Hanoverian period waste lands were enclosed, the slate mines of the north and the coal pits of the south were opened.

The Tudors succeeded in getting the upper classes to speak English, and to turn their backs on Welsh life. The peasant was left supreme: he knew not what to do at first, but light soon came.

Pass through Wales, and you will see the life of both periods—the ruined castles and the ruined monasteries of the old; the quarries and pits, the towns and ports, the churches and chapels, the schools and colleges of the present.

CHAPTER XXI: HOWEL HARRIS

It is difficult to write about religion without giving offence. Religion will come into politics, and must come into history. It has given much, perhaps most, of its strength to modern Wales; it has given it many, if not most, of its political difficulties.

There are periods of religious calm and periods of religious fervour in the life of every nation. I do not know whether it is necessary, but it is certainly the fact—the two periods condemn each other with great energy. With regard to creed—the life of religion—you will find that the periods of energy tend to be Calvinistic—an intense belief that man is a mere instrument in the hands of God, working out plans he does not understand; while in periods of rest it tends to be Arminian—a comfortable belief that man sees his future clearly, and that he can guide it as he likes. With regard to the Church—the body of religion—it is fortunate, in times of calm, if it is established, to keep the spirit of religion alive; it is fortunate, in times of fervour, if it is free, in order that the new life may give it a more perfect shape.

Now we must remember that there can be no calm without a little indifference, and that there can be no enthusiasm without a little intolerance. So men call each other fanatics and bigots and hypocrites, because they have not taken the trouble to realise that there is much variety in human character and in the workings of the human mind. Perhaps it is also worth remembering that an institution is not placed at the mercy of a reformer, but gradually changed.

The eighteenth century was a century of indifference in religion in Wales, the nineteenth century was a century of enthusiasm. The Church at the beginning of the eighteenth century, at any rate as far as the higher clergy were concerned, was apathetic to religion, and alive only to selfish interests. The Whig bishops were appointed for political reasons; they hated the Tory principles of the Welsh squires, and they neglected and despised the Welsh people they had never tried to understand. In England, the Defoes and the Swifts of literature were encouraged and utilised by the political parties; in Wales, where clergymen were the only writers, the Whig bishops distrusted them, and silenced them where they could, because they wrote Welsh. The Church did not show more misapplication of revenue than the State, perhaps; but, while the people could not leave the State as a protest against corruption, they could leave the Church. And, during the middle of the eighteenth century, a great national awakening began.

The trumpet blast of the awakening was Howel Harris. He was a Breconshire peasant, of strong passion which became sanctified by a life-long struggle, of devouring ambition which he nearly succeeded in taming to a life of intense service to God. Many bitter things have been said about him, but nothing more bitter than he has said about himself in the volumes of prayers and recriminations he wrote to torture his own soul, and to goad himself into harder work. The fame of his eloquence filled the land, and districts expected his appearance anxiously, as in old times they expected Owen Glendower. Howel Harris was, however, no political agitator. He had an imperious will, and he wished to rule his brethren; he was aggressive and military in spirit; God to him was the Lord of Hosts; he preached the gospel of peace in the uniform of an officer of the militia, and he sent many of his converts to fight abroad in the battles of the century. He had a love of organisation; he established at Trevecca what was partly a religious community, and partly a co-operative manufacturing company. But, wherever he stood to proclaim the wrath of God, no shower of stones or condemnation of minister or justice could make those who heard him forget him, or believe that what he said was wrong.

If I were writing for antiquarians, and not for those who read history in order to see why things are now as they are, I would write details—important and instructive—about the Church of the eighteenth century, and about the congregations of Dissenters which the seventeenth century handed over to the eighteenth to persecute and despise. The Independents and Baptists sturdily maintained their principles of religious liberty, but they found the century a stiff-necked one, and their congregations were content with merely existing. The Quakers maintained that war was wrong while Britain passed through war fever after war fever—the Seven Years' War and the wars against Napoleon. Howel Harris' voice might have been a voice crying in the wilderness, if it had not been for the spiritual life of the existing congregations, conformist and dissenting. Modern ideas in Wales have been profoundly affected by the Quakers, and especially in districts from which, as a sect, they have long passed away.

The voice of Howel Harris called all these to a new life; and it is about that new life, in the variety given it by all the different actors in it, that I want you to think now. It made preaching necessary, for one thing; and it was followed by a century of great pulpit oratory. It profoundly affected literature. It gave Wales, to begin with, a hymn literature that no country in the world has surpassed. The contrast between the Reformation and the Revival is very striking—one gave the people a Church government established by law and a literature of translations, the other gave it institutions of its own making and original living thought. The Revival gave literature in every branch a new strength and greater wealth.

It created a demand for education. Griffith Jones of Llanddowror established a system of circulating schools, the teachers moving from place to place as a room was offered them—sometimes a church and sometimes a barn. Charles of Bala established a system of Sunday Schools, and the whole nation gradually joined it. The Press became active, newspapers appeared. It became quite clear that a new life throbbed in the land.

CHAPTER XXII: THE REFORM ACTS

The new life brought an inevitable demand for a share in the government of the country, and this brought the old order and the new face to face. The political power was entirely in the hands of the squires, alienated from the peasants in many cases by a difference of language, and in most cases by a difference of religion.

The Act of 1535 had, as we have seen, given Wales a representation in Parliament. Each shire had one member only; except Monmouth, which had two. Each shire town had one member, except that of Merioneth; and Haverfordwest was given a member. The county franchise was the forty shilling freehold; it therefore excluded not only those who had no connection with the land, but the copyholder—who was really a landowner, but whose tenure was regarded as base, on account of his villein origin. This copyholder was undoubtedly the descendant of the Welsh serf of mediæval times.

The first Reform Act, that of 1832, was won for the great manufacturing towns of England, but Wales benefited by it. It extended the franchise to the copyholder, and to the farmer paying £50 rent, in the counties; it gave the towns a uniform £10 household franchise. It also brought many of the towns into the system of representation. It raised the number of members from twenty-seven to thirty-two; the agricultural districts getting two, and the mining districts two.

The slight change in representation is a recognition of the growing industries of the country, especially in the coal and iron districts. The coal of the great coalfield of South Wales had been worked as far back as Norman times; but it was in the nineteenth century that the coal and iron industries of South Wales, and the coal and slate industries of North Wales became important. Cardiff, Swansea, and Newport became important ports; and places that few had ever heard of before—like Ystradyfodwg or Blaenau Ffestiniog—became the centres of important industries. But, in 1832, Wales was still mainly pastoral and agricultural; and the Act, though it did much for the towns, left the representation of the counties in the hands of the same class. Still, it was the towns that showed disappointment, as was seen in the Chartism of the wool district of Llanidloes and of the coal district of Newport.

The second Reform Act, of 1867, gave Merthyr Tydvil two representatives instead of one, otherwise it left the distribution of seats as it had been before. But the new extension of the franchise—to the borough householder, the borough £10 lodger, and especially the £12 tenant farmer—gave new classes political power. It was followed by a fierce struggle between the old landed gentry and their tenants, a struggle which was moderated to a certain extent by the Ballot Act of 1870, and by the great migration of the country population to the slate and coal districts.

The rapid rise of the importance of the industrial districts is seen in the third Reform Act of 1885. The country districts represented by the small boroughs of the agricultural counties of Brecon, Cardigan, Pembroke, and Anglesey, were wholly or partly disfranchised. But the slate county of Carnarvonshire had an additional member; and in the coal and iron country, Swansea and Carmarthenshire and Monmouthshire had one additional member each, and Glamorgan three.

The third Reform Act enfranchised the agricultural labourer and the country artisan. In England many doubts were expressed about the intelligence or the colour of the politics of the new voter; but, in Wales, most would admit that he was as intelligent as any voter enfranchised before him; all knew there could be no doubt about his politics.

The character of the representation of Wales has entirely changed. The squire gave place to the capitalist, and the capitalist to popular leaders. Wales, whose people blindly followed the gentry in the Great Civil War, is now the most democratic part of Britain.

CHAPTER XXIII: EDUCATION

The chief feature of the history of Wales during the eighteenth and nineteenth centuries is the growth of a system of education.

The most democratic, the most perfect, and the most efficient method is still that of the Sunday School. It was well established before the death of Charles of Bala, whose name is most closely connected with it, in 1814. It soon became, and it still remains, a school for the whole people, from children to patriarchs. Its language is that of its district. Its teachers are selected for efficiency—they are easily shifted to the classes which they can teach best; and, if not successful, they go back willingly to the "teachers' class," where all are equal. The reputation of a good Sunday School teacher is still the highest degree that can be won in Wales. Plentiful text books of high merit, and an elaborate system of oral and written examinations, mark the last stage in its development.

The Literary Meeting is a kind of secular Sunday School. The rules of alliterative poetry and the study of Welsh literature and history, and sometimes of more general knowledge, take the place of the study of Jewish history, and psalm, and gospel. The Literary Meetings feed the Eisteddvod.

The Eisteddvod passed through the same phases as the nation. It was an aspect of the court of the prince during the Middle Ages. In Tudor times it was used partly to please the people, but chiefly to regulate the bards by forcing them to qualify for a degree—a sure method of moderating their patriotism and of diminishing their number. In modern times the Eisteddvod is a great democratic meeting, and it is the most characteristic of all Welsh institutions. Its chairing of the bards is an ancient ceremony; its gorsedd of bards is probably modern. But the people themselves still remain the judges of poetry; they care very little whether a poet has won a chair or not, while a gorsedd degree probably does him more harm than good.

Elementary education, in its modern sense, began with the circulating schools of Griffith Jones of Llanddowror in 1730. They were exceedingly successful because the instruction was given in Welsh, and they stopped after teaching 150,000 to read not because there was no demand for them, but on account of a dispute about their endowments in 1779, eighteen years after Griffith Jones' death. They were followed by voluntary schools, very often kept by illiterate teachers.

Between 1846 and 1848 two organisations—the Welsh Education Committee and the Cambrian Society—were formed; and they developed, respectively, the national schools and the British schools. After the Education Act of 1870, the schools became voluntary or Board; education gradually became compulsory and free; and in 1902 an attempt was made to give the whole system a unity and to connect it with the ordinary system of local government.

The training of teachers became a matter of the highest importance. In 1846 a college for this purpose was established at Brecon, and then removed to Swansea. From 1848 to 1862, colleges were established at Carmarthen, Carnarvon, and Bangor.

The history of secondary education is longer. It was served, after the dissolution of the monasteries, by endowed schools—like that of the Friars at Bangor—and by proprietary schools. By the Education Act of 1889, a complete system of secondary schools, under popular control, was established. Two of the endowed schools still remain—Brecon, founded by the religionists of the Reformation, and Llandovery, the Welsh school founded by a patriot of modern times.

It was principally for the ministry of religion that secondary schools and colleges were first established. Schools were founded in many districts, and important colleges at Lampeter (degree-granting), Carmarthen, Brecon, Bala, Trevecca, Pontypool, Llangollen, Haverfordwest. Many of these have a long history.

Higher education had been the dream of many centuries. Owen Glendower had thought of establishing two new universities at the beginning of the period of the Revival of Letters; among his supporters were many of the Welsh students who led in the great faction fights of mediæval Oxford. Oliver Cromwell and Richard Baxter had thought of Welsh higher education. But nothing was done. In the eighteenth century, and in the nineteenth until 1870, the Test Act shut the doors of the old Universities to most Welshmen; the new University of London did not teach, it only examined; the Scotch Universities, to which Welsh students crowded, were very far. In 1872, chiefly through the exertions of Sir Hugh Owen, the University College of Wales was opened at Aberystwyth, and maintained for ten years by support from the people. The Government helped, and two new colleges were added—the University College of South Wales at Cardiff in 1883, and the University College of North Wales at Bangor in 1884. In 1893 Queen Victoria gave a charter which formed the three colleges into the University of Wales. Lord Aberdare, its first Chancellor, lived to see it in thorough working order. On Lord Aberdare's death, the Prince of Wales was elected Chancellor in 1896; and when he ascended the throne in 1901, the present Prince of Wales became Chancellor.

The tendency of the whole system of Welsh education is towards greater unity. There is a dual government of the secondary schools and of the colleges, the one by the Central Board and the other by the University Court—a historical accident which is now a blemish on the system. The Training Colleges are still outside the University, but they are gravitating rapidly towards it. The theological colleges are necessarily independent, but the University offers their students a course in arts, so that they can specialise on theology and its kindred subjects. The ideal system is: an efficient and patriotic University regulating the whole work of the secondary and elementary schools, guided by the willingness of the County Councils, or of an education authority appointed by them, to provide means.

The rise of the educational system is the most striking and the most interesting chapter in Welsh history. But the facts are so numerous and the development is so sudden that, in spite of one, it becomes a mere list of acts and dates.

CHAPTER XXIV: LOCAL GOVERNMENT

The French Revolution was condemned by Britain, and the voices raised in its favour in Wales were few. The excesses of the Revolution, and the widespread fear of a Napoleonic invasion, caused a strong reaction against progress. The years immediately after were years of great suffering, but the very suffering prepared the way for the progress of the future, because it made men willing to leave their own districts and to move into the coal and slate districts, where wages were high enough to enable them to live.

The first demand was for political enfranchisement. In 1832, in 1867, and in 1884 the franchise was extended, and every interest found a voice in Parliament. But, with the exception of the sharp struggle between the tenant and landlord after the Reform Act of 1867, the effects of enfranchisement on Wales have been very few. Two Acts alone have been passed as purely Welsh Acts—the Sunday Closing Act, and the Intermediate Education Act. In Parliament, the voice of Wales is weak even though unanimous; it can be outvoted by the capital or by four English provincial towns. Until quite recently its semi-independence—due to geography and past history—was looked upon as a source of weakness to the Empire rather than of strength. Its love for the past appeals to the one political party, its desire for progress to the other, but its distinctive ideals and its separate language are looked upon, at the very least, as political misfortunes. Education and justice have suffered from official want of toleration; the appointment of a County Court judge who could not speak Welsh, within living memory, has been justified by Government on the ground that Englishmen resident in Wales object to being tried by a Welsh judge.

Far more important to Wales than the Reform Acts are the Local Government Acts which followed them. When the Reform Act of 1884 added the agricultural labourer to the electors of representatives in Parliament, every interest had a voice. A further extension of the franchise would not affect the balance of parties, it was thought; and a British Parliament has no time or desire to think of sentiment or theoretical perfection. The Parliament found it had too much to do, the multiplicity of interests made it impossible to pay effective attention to them. The result has been that half a century of extension of the franchise has been followed by half a century of extension of local government. The County Council Act came in 1888, and the Local Government Act in 1894.

Of all parts of Britain, Wales had least local government, and needed most. Its justices of the peace were alien in religion, race, and sympathy; they were either country squires who had lost touch with the people, or English and Scotch capitalists who, with rare exceptions, took no trouble to understand the people they governed, or to learn their language. The vestry meeting had been active enough during the early part of the eighteenth century; but religious difficulties made it impossible for a semi-ecclesiastical institution to represent a parish. The Tudor policy had separated the people from the greater land-owners; the iron masters and coal-owners had not yet become part of the people; there was not a single institution except the Eisteddvod where all classes met.

In no part of the country was local government so warmly welcomed, and no part of the country was more ready for it. One thing the peasants had been allowed to do—they could build schools and colleges, churches and chapels. They had filled the country with these—their architecture, finance, government, are those of the peasant. The religious revivals had left organisers and institutions. Four or five religious bodies had a system of institutions—parish, district, county, central. All these were thoroughly democratic in character. When the Local Government Acts were passed, there was hardly a Welshman of full age and average ability who had not been a delegate or in authority; and those of striking ability, if they could afford the time, continually sat in some little council or other and watched over the interests of some institution.

It was from among these trained men that the councillors for the new county, district, and parish senates were elected. The work of the councils, especially that of the County Council, has been very difficult; and when the time comes to write their history, the historian will have to set himself to explain why the first councils were served by men who had extraordinary tact for government and great skill in financial matters. In the lower councils the village Hampden's eloquence is modified by the chilling responsibility for the rates, but the Parish Councils have already, in many places, made up for the negligence of generations of sleepy magistrates and officials.

With a great difference, it is true, Wales under local government is Wales back again in the times of the princes. The parish is roughly the maenol, the district is the commote or the cantrev, the shire is the little kingdom—like Ceredigion or Morgannwg—which fought so sturdily against any attempt to subject it.

The local councils were fortunate in the time of their appearance. They came at a period characterised by an intense desire for a better system of education, and at a time of rapidly growing prosperity. A heavy rate was possible, and the people were willing to bear it. The County Councils were able to build over seventy intermediate schools within a few years; and that at a time when both elementary and higher education made heavy demands on what was still a comparatively poor county. The District Councils were able to lower the amount of outdoor relief considerably, and without causing any real hardship, for they had knowledge of their districts as well as the philanthropy that comes naturally to man when he grants other people's money. The Parish Councils have become the guardians of public paths; they have begun to provide parish libraries, and the little parish senate educates its constituency and brings its wisdom to bear upon a number of practical questions, such as cottage gardens and fairs.

CHAPTER XXV: THE WALES OF TODAY

The most striking characteristic of the Wales of today is its unity—self-conscious and self-reliant. The presence of this unity is felt by all, though it may be explained in different ways. It cannot be explained by race; for the population of the west midlands and the north of England, possibly of the whole of it, have been made up of the same elements. It cannot be explained by language—nearly one half of the Welsh people speak no Welsh. Some attribute it to the inexorable laws of geography and climate, others to the fatalism of history. Others frivolously put it down to modern football. But no one who knows Wales is ignorant of it.

The modern unity of the Welsh people—seen occasionally in a function of the University, or at a national Eisteddvod, or in a conference of the County Councils—has become a fact in spite of many difficulties.

One difficulty has been the absence of a capital. The office of the University and the National Museum are at Cardiff, in the extreme south; the National Library is at Aberystwyth, on the western sea. The thriving industries, the densely populated districts, and the frequent and active railways, are in the extreme south or in the extreme north; and they are separated by five or six shires of pastures and sheep-runs, without large towns, and with comparatively few railways. In the three southern counties—Glamorgan, Monmouth, and Carmarthen—the population is between two and six people to 10 acres, and the industrial population is from twelve to three times the number of the agricultural. In the central counties—Brecon, Radnor, Cardigan, Merioneth, Montgomery—the population is below one for 10 acres; the industrial and agricultural population are about equal, except in Radnor, where the agricultural is more than two to one. Though Merioneth has more sheep even than Brecon—and each of them has nearly 400,000—its industrial population, owing to the slate districts, is double the agricultural. The population begins to thicken again as we get nearer the slate, limestone, and coal districts. In Denbigh it is two to the 10 acres, in Carnarvon it is three, and in Flint it rises to four or five. In these northern counties the industrial population is double or treble the agricultural. The fertile western counties of Pembroke and Anglesey come between the industrial and grazing counties in density of population. [4]

Unity has arisen in spite of differences caused by the intensity of a religious revival, an intensity that periodically renews its strength. The Welsh are divided into sects, and the bitterness of sectarian differences occasionally invades politics and education. But there are two ever-present antidotes. One is the Welsh sense of humour, the nearest relative or the best friend of toleration. The other is the hymn—creed has been turned into song, and that is at least half way to turning it into life; the heresy hunter is disarmed by the poetry of the hymn, and its music has charms to soothe the sectarian breast. The co-operation of all in the work of local government has also enlarged sympathy.

Unity has arisen in spite of the bilingual difficulty. Rather more than one half of the people now habitually speak English. For three centuries an Act—a dead letter from the beginning—ordered all Government officials to speak English; for many generations, until recently, Welsh children were not taught Welsh in schools, and they could not be taught English. The bilingual difficulty is now at an end. The two languages are taught in the schools, and as living languages. It is clear, on the one hand, that every one should learn English, the language of the Empire and of commerce. It is also clear that, on account of its own beauty as well as that of the great literature it enshrines, Welsh should be taught in every school throughout Wales.

Next to its unity, a characteristic of modern Wales is its democratic feeling. It is a country with a thoughtful and intelligent peasantry, and it is a country without a middle class. There is a very small upper class—the old Welsh land-owning families who once, before they turned their backs on Welsh literature, led the country. They have never been hated or despised, they are simply ignored. Their tendency now is to come into touch with the people, and they are always welcomed. But a middle class, in the English sense, does not exist. The wealthier industrial class is bound by the closest ties of sympathy to the farmer and labourer. The farmer's holding is generally small—from 50 to 250 acres—and he always treats his servants and labourers as equals.

The three great levelling causes—religion, industry, [5] and education—have been at work in Wales in recent years. Education helps and is helped by equality. In town and country alike all Welsh children attend the same schools—elementary and secondary; and they proceed, those that do proceed, to the same University, and a university is essentially a levelling institution. The dialects, as well as the literary language, are recognised; and no dialect has a stigma. In this respect Wales is more like Scotland than England.

There is one other characteristic of modern Wales—a certain pride, not so much in what has been done, but in what is going to be done. Wales is small, though not much smaller than Palestine, or Holland, or Switzerland, and every part of it knows the other. There is a healthy rivalry between its towns and between its colleges; each town can show that it has done something for Wales in the past—by means of its industries, or school, or press. In the strong feeling of unity there is ambition to surpass, and each part lives in the light of the action of the other parts.

The day is a day of incessant activity—industrial, educational, literary, and political. What is true in the life of the individual is true in the life of a nation—a day of hard work is a happy day and a day of hope.

An outline of Welsh history

INFLUENCES UNDER WHICH THE HISTORY OF WALES WAS FORMED

1. The nature of its rocks—Igneous, Cambrian, Silurian, Old Red Sandstone, Limestone, Coal—all belonging to the Primary Period. Its rocks

(a) explain its scenery;

(b) explain its wealth, the richest part of Britain in minerals.

2. The configuration of its surface.

(a) It is isolated, its mountains being surrounded by the sea, or rising sharply from the plains. It is part of the range of mountains which runs along the whole of the west coast of Britain; but the range is broken at the mouth of the Severn and at the mouth of the Dee.

(b) It is divided, its valleys and roads radiating in all directions. So we have in its history

A. Wars of Independence.

B. Civil War.

THE PEOPLE WHO CAME INTO WALES

1. The Iberians—a general name for the short dark people who still form the greater part of the nations. They had stone weapons, and lived in tribes; they became subject to later invaders, but gradually became free. Their language is lost.

2. The Celts—a tall fair-haired race, speaking an Aryan tongue. It was their migration that was stopped by the rise of Rome. Four groups of mountains, four nations (Celtic and Iberian), four mediæval kingdoms, and four modern dioceses can be remembered thus:

i.

Snowdonia

Decangi

Gwynedd

Bangor

ii.

Berwyn

Ordovices

Powys

St Asaph
iii.
Plinlimmon
Demetae
Dyved
St David's
iv.
Black Mountains
Silures
Morgannwg
Llandaff
3. The Romans. They made roads, built cities, worked mines.
50–78.
The Conquest. The Silures were defeated in 50, the Decangi in 58, the Ordovices in 78.
80–200.
The Settlement. Wales part of a Roman province including Chester and York.
200–450.
The struggle against the new wandering nations. The introduction of Christianity.
450–
The House of Cunedda represents Roman rule.
4. The English.
577.
Battle of Deorham. Wales separated from Cornwall.
613.
Battle of Chester. Wales separated from Cumbria.

I. THE WALES OF THE PRINCES

Isolated after the battles of Deorham and Chester, mediæval Wales begins to make its own history. The House of Cunedda represents unity, the other princes represent independence. English, Danish, Norman attacks from without.

1.
613–1063.
The struggle between the Welsh princes and the English provincial kings. From the battle of Chester to the fall of Griffith ap Llywelyn.

(a) Between Wales and Northumbria, 613–700; for the sovereignty of the north. Cadwallon, Cadwaladr v. Edwin, Oswald, Oswiu.

(b) Between Wales and Mercia, 700–815; for the valley of the Severn. Rhodri Molwynog and his sons v. Ethelbald and Offa.

(c) Between Wales and the Danes, 815–1000. Rhodri the Great and Howel the Good.

(d) Between Wales and Wessex, 1000–1063; for political influence. Griffith ap Llywelyn v. Harold.
2.
1063–1284.
The struggle between the Welsh princes and the central English kings.
(a)
1066–1137.
The Norman Conquest. Norman barons v. Griffith ap Conan and Griffith ap Rees.
1063.
Bleddyn of Powys tries to unite Wales.
1070.
William the Conqueror at Chester. Advance of Norman barons from Chester, Shrewsbury, Hereford, Gloucester.
1075.
Death of Bleddyn; succeeded by Trahaiarn.
1077.
Battle of Mynydd Carn. Restoration of House of Cunedda—Griffith ap Conan in the north; Rees, followed by his son Griffith, in the south.
1094.
Norman castles dominate Powys, Gwent, Morgannwg, and Dyved. Gwynedd and Deheubarth threatened.
1137.
Death of Griffith ap Conan and Griffith ap Rees, after setting bounds to the Norman Conquest.
(b)
1137–1197.
The struggle against Henry II. and his sons.
1137.
The accession of Owen Gwynedd and of the Lord Rees of the Deheubarth.

1157.

Henry II. interferes in the quarrel of Owen and Cadwaladr.

1564.

The Cistercians at Strata Florida.

1164.

Meeting of Owen Gwynedd, the Lord Rees, and Owen Cyveiliog at Corwen, to oppose Henry II.

1170.

Death of Owen Gwynedd.

1188.

Preaching of the Crusades in Wales.

1189.

Death of Henry II.

1197.

Death of the Lord Rees.

(c)

1194–1240.

The reign of Llywelyn the Great.

1194–1201.

Securing the crown of Gwynedd.

1201–1208.

Alliance with King John.

1208–1212.

War with John.

1212–1218.

Alliance with barons of Magna Carta.

1218–1226.

Struggle with the Marshalls of Pembroke.

1226–1240.

Unity of Wales: alliance with Marshalls.

(d)

1240–1284.

The Wars of Independence.

1241.

David II. does homage to Henry III.

1244.

Death of Griffith, in trying to escape from the Tower of London.

1245.

Fierce fighting on the Conway.

1254.

Edward (afterwards Edward I.) Earl of Chester.

1255.

Llywelyn ap Griffith supreme in Gwynedd.

1263.

Alliance with the English barons.

1267.

Treaty of Montgomery; Llywelyn Prince of Wales.

1274.

Llywelyn refuses to do homage to Edward I.

1277.

Treaty of Rhuddlan; Llywelyn keeps Gwynedd only.

1278.

Llywelyn marries Eleanor de Montfort.

1282.

Last war. Battle of Moel y Don. Llywelyn's death.

1284.

Statute of Wales.

3.

1284–1535.

The rule of sheriff and march lord.

1287.

Revolt of Ceredigion.

1294.

Revolts In Gwynedd, Dyved, Morgannwg.

1315.

Revolt of Llywelyn Bren.

1349.

The Black Death in Wales.

1400.

Rise of Owen Glendower.

1402.

Battles of the Vyrnwy and Bryn Glas.

1404.

Anti-Welsh legislation.

1455.

The Wars of the Roses.

1461.

Battle of Mortimer's Cross.

1468.

Siege of Harlech.

1469.

Battle of Edgecote.

1478.

Court of Wales at Ludlow.

1485.

Battle of Bosworth and accession of Henry VII.

1535.

Act of Union. All Wales governed by king through sheriffs.

II. THE WALES OF THE PEOPLE.

In 1535 the march lordships were formed into shires, and a reign of law began.

1535–1603.

Period of loyalty to Tudor sovereigns—for equality before law and political rights.

1536.

The march lordships become shire ground. Wales given a representation in Parliament, and its own system of law courts—the Great Sessions of Wales.

1539.

Welsh passive resistance to the Reformation.

1567.

Sir Thomas Middleton opens silver mines of Cardiganshire.

1588.

Bishop Morgan's Welsh Bible.

1593.

Execution of John Penry.

Results:

1. Destruction of power of barons.

2. Anglicising of gentry.

3. A Welsh Bible.

1603–1689.

Struggle between new and old ideas.

1618.

Coal of South Wales attracts attention.

1640.

First Civil War.

1644.

Brereton and Myddleton win North Wales, Laugharne and Poyer win South Wales, for Parliament.

1648.

Second Civil War: siege of Pembroke.

1650.

Puritan "Act for the better Propagation of the Gospel in Wales."

1670.

Vavasour Powell dies in prison.

1689.

Abolition of the Court of Wales.

1689–1894.

Rise of the Welsh democracy.

1719.

Copper works at Swansea.

1730.

Griffith Jones' circulating schools.

1750.

Iron furnaces at Merthyr Tydvil.

1773.

Death of Howel Harris.

1814.

Death of Charles of Bala.

1830.

Abolition of Great Sessions of Wales.

1832.

First Reform Bill.

1839.

Chartism at Llanidloes and Newport.

1867.

Second Reform Bill.

1872, 1883, 1884.

University Colleges.

1884.

Third Reform Bill.

1888.

County Council Act.

1889.

Secondary Education Act.

1894.

Local Government Act. University of Wales.

FOOTNOTES

[1] Mihangel=Michael. Llan Fihangel = Si Michael's.

[2] Mair=Mary. Llan Fair=St Mary's.

[3] About 1291 the abbeys of Aberconway and Strata Marcella had over a hundred cows each, Whitland over a thousand sheep, and Basingwerk over two thousand.

[4] According to the census of 1901 the population per square mile of Glamorgan is 758, Monmouth 427, Carmarthen 141, Brecon 73, Radnor 49, Cardigan 88, Montgomery 68, Merioneth 74, Denbigh 197, Carnarvon 217, Flint 319, Pembroke 143, Anglesey 183.

The rate of increase per cent. between 1891 and 1901 are—Wales 13.3; England 12.1; Scotland 11.1; Ireland—5.2.

[5] In 1801 the population of Cardiff was 1870, and coal was brought down from Merthyr on donkeys. In 1901 the three ports of Cardiff, Newport, and Swansea exported nearly as much coal as all the great English and Scotch ports put together.

[109] In the book this "appendix" is inserted at page 109, where it doesn't fit and is in the middle of paragraph. It's been moved to an appendix in this eText.—DP.

[135] This table contains the following genealogy. (For items with an asterisk: the links between the House of Cunedda and the three ruling families after the Norman Conquest rest on the authority of tradition rather than on that of records.)

Cunedda Wledig (Dux Britanniae). Maelgwn Gwynedd. Cadwaladr.

Then Idwal.

Then Rhodri Molwynog.

Then Conan Tindaethwy.

Then Esyllt=Mervin.

Then Rhodri the Great who had issue: Anarawd, Cadell and Mervin.

Anarawd had issue Idwal the Bald who had issue Iago then (?) Conan* (See Table II.).

Cadwell had issue Howel the Good who had issue Owen.

Owen had issue Einion who had issue Cadwell and Meredith.

Cadwell had issue Tewdwr* (See Table III.)

Meredith had issue Angharad*.

Angharad = Llywelyn ab Seisyllt and had issue Griffith.

Angharad = Cynvyn who had issue Bleddyn and Rhiwallon (See Table IV.)

[136a] This table contains the following genealogy:

Griffith ap Conan had issue Owen Gwynedd, Cadwaladr and Gwenllian = G. ap Rees.

Owen Gwynedd had issue Iorwerth and David I.

Iorwerth had issue Llywelyn the Great.

Llywelyn the Great had issue Griffith and David II.

Griffith had issue Llywelyn the Last, Owen the Red, David and Rhodri.

Llywelyn the Last = Eleanor de Montfort and had issue Gwenllian.

Rhodri had issue Thomas who had issue Owen of Wales.

[136b] This table contains the following genealogy:

Rees ap Tudor had issue Griffith and Nest.

Griffith had issue The Lord Rees.

The Lord Rees had issue Griffith and Rees the Hoarse.

[137] This table contains the following genealogy:

Bleddyn ap Cynvyn had issue Meredith, Cadwgan and Iorwerth.

Cadwgan had issue Owen of Powys.

Meredith had issue Madoc and Owen Cyveiliog.

Owen Cyveiliog had issue Griffith who had issue Gwenwynwyn.

Madoc had issue Griffith Maelor who had issue Madoc who had issue Griffith of Bromfield.

Griffith of Bromfield had issue Madoc and Griffith Vychan.

Griffith Vychan had issue Madoc who had issue Griffith who had issue Griffith Vychan who had issue Owen Glendower.

[138] This table contains the following genealogy:

Llywelyn the Great had issue Gladys the Dark=Ralph Mortimer of Wigmore.

Gladys the Dark and Ralph Mortimer of Wigmore had issue Roger Mortimer = Matilda de Braose.

Roger Mortimer and Matilda de Braose had issue Edmund and Roger of Chirk.

Edmund had issue Roger, first Earl of March, who had issue Edmund who had issue Roger, second Earl of March, who had issue Edmund, third Earl of March=Philipa.

Edmund, third Earl of March and Philipa had issue Roger and Edmund = d. of Glendower.

Roger had issue Edmund and Anne=Richard, Earl of Cambridge (see later).

On a different line: Edward III. had issue Lionel of Clarence, John of Gaunt and Edmund of York.

Edmund of York had issue Richard, Earl of Cambridge=Anne.

The lines then merge with Anne=Richard, Earl of Cambridge who had issue Richard, Duke of York (killed at Wakefield, 1460).

Richard, Duke of York had issue Edward IV, and Richard III. (killed at Bosworth, 1485).

Edward IV. had issue Elizabeth = Henry VII.

Henry VII. and Elizabeth had issue Henry VIII.

[139] This table contains the following genealogy:

Edward III. had issue John of Gaunt who had issue Henry IV. and John Beaufort I. Earl of Somerset.

Henry IV. = Catherine of France had issue Henry VI.

Catherine of France = Owen Tudor had issue Edmund Tudor, Earl of Richmond=Margaret Beaufort who had issue Henry VII. who had issue Henry VIII. who had issue Edward VI., Mary and Elizabeth.

John Beaufort I. Earl of Somerset had issue John Beaufort II., Duke of Somerset who had issue Margaret Beaufort (see above).